CREATING STRATEGIC INNOVATION

ESOP Version

Achieving Profitable Growth & Innovation Through Competency Development & Action Plans

The Workbook for Teamwork

JACK VEALE

*With much help
from my clients,
mentors, and friends*

TABLE OF CONTENTS

Introduction. 5

chapter 1: Creating a Team System 13

chapter 2: Building Team Decision Skills 31

chapter 3: Developing Problem Solving Skills - Part 1 43

chapter 4: Developing Problem Solving Skills - Part 2 61

chapter 5: Customer Requirements 79

chapter 6: Measurements & Scorecards 91

chapter 7: Implementing Change. 109

chapter 8: The Business Life Cycle 121

chapter 9: Management Concepts 135

chapter 10: The Management Process 149

chapter 11: Personal Development 173

chapter 12: ESOPs – Basic Terminology & Concepts 195

chapter 13: Getting Results 209

index 220

sources 226

checklist 228

Original design and typesetting by Susan Hannah.

Published by PTCFO, Inc. dba: Green Mountain Leadership Institute
48 Walkley Rd
West Hartford, Connecticut USA 06119-1345
www.ptcfo.com (860) 232-9858 Fax (860) 232-9438

ISBN: 978-0-9747663-5-5

ACKNOWLEDGMENT

I want to thank my "best friend for life," Laurie, and my boys for putting up with the loss of my time spent away from each other in order to do the research and complete this book. I love you very much!

There were many individuals who assisted me in this process. A special thanks to Drs. Richard Hansen, PhD and Hubert Maultsby, PhD for taking the time to edit the script and provide meaningful input to the development of this workbook. My partner, Bill Kenney, also provided help when we updated it in 2005. I also want to recognize my book designer, Susan Hannah, who brutalized me with her great ideas and changes for this new design. If it wasn't for Amy Viscio and Jonathan Moffly for insulting me so badly about my old book, this would have never happened! All three deserve my sincere gratitude!

And a sincere appreciation to my special friends and/or clients; Bill Fischbeck, Dick Wirth, Phil Cahill, Bill Pape, Al Torrisi, and Marshall Jespersen who were so helpful in motivating me to complete this book. Without their wisdom, support, and encouragement, this book would have never been realized. Others who were influential with developing this book include the people of Strahman Valves, Jackson Lumber Millwork, and Drs. Jody Locklear, PhD, and Rich Schneider, PhD.

Photo and Illustration Credits: Cover photo & pg 7: ©Yuri_Acurs|Dreamstime.com; pg 21: ©Les Cunliffe|Dreamstime.com; pg 35: ©Andrey Kiselev|Dreamstime.com; pg 47: ©Feng Yu|Dreamstime.com; pg 51: ©Dadek|Dreamstime.com; pg 65: ©Monika Wisniewska|Dreamstime.com; pg 80: ©Yvanovich|Dreamstime.com; pg 81: ©Jbouzou|Dreamstime.com; pg 102: ©Icofoto|Dreamstime.com; pg 115: ©Pryzmat|Dreamstime.com; pg 215: ©Maigi|Dreamstime.com; pg 216: ©Absolut_photos|Dreamstime.com; pg 152: ©Nikolai Sorokin|Dreamstime.com

INTRODUCTION

Over the years, we have found that businesses hit a glass ceiling on revenue growth due to many factors. Companies are finding that the competitive models of scale are no longer as important as information and ideas. CEO's can only make a limited amount of decisions, due to factors of time, available information, and the pace by which decisions are now being made. Organizations are frightened by the prospect of changing their business models frequently. Why? To change an organization once is extremely hard and difficult; to do so more than once requires new ways of thinking and doing things.

Implementing a Strategic Plan, or developing innovation can be very difficult if skills or organizational competencies are not developed deep into the organization. Every organization is facing rapid declines in transaction costs that, in the past, only the large scale companies enjoyed. The internet is broadening the supply of information interactively. The recently developed ISO 9000 standards are forcing change in many industries. As a result, strategic contests are not just about resources (the strong vs. the weak), but also about ideas as a competitive advantage.

One of the key restraining factors is the organization's ability to solve simple and complex problems effectively. Another is the lack of communication and information sharing systems that improves individual and group performance by building and sharing knowledge. The Creating Strategic Innovation (CSI) Workbook attempts to help to explain the successful dynamics of an organization with the goal of implementing management systems consisting of high performance management teams with superior problem-solving abilities.

In addition, we have found that requiring people to take home homework after a busy day can sometimes create hardships. We also have learned that not everyone learns by reading; many learn by listening. FDR and LBJ were two U.S. presidents who acquired information by presentation, not by the written word. Thus, they surrounded themselves with key people who were speakers, not writers. JFK and Jimmy Carter, on the other hand, were avid readers, requiring detailed reports rather than oral presentations. Their cabinet consisted of detailed writers rather than oral speakers.

For that reason, we have tried to keep the reading easy by employing a larger print size, providing graphs, charts, handouts, and exercises to learn from, and forms to help in the implementation. Yes, there is homework, but not much of it. Continuous improvement involves *your ability* to implement effective change in areas where you have control. Doing homework will help speed up your ability to perform more effectively.

The use of the CSI workbook will teach the reader a process by which to share knowledge. Traditionally, people value things that are scarce. While information has been something hoarded to create value, we believe it is worth more shared than hoarded. Creating a learning process requires that people who are genuinely interested in helping each other develop the capacity for action and sharing information and/or ideas.

We do understand that each organization has its own way of doing things. Our approach is to teach you, the reader, to recognize and magnify those valued competencies that have allowed your company to grow in the past, while "shoring up" those weaknesses that can restrain a company from meeting and surpassing the marketplace's challenges.

A much bantered about concept is TQM or "Total Quality Management." TQM represents a body of knowledge and systems that enable a management team to improve quality and profitability. "Kaizen" in Japanese means, "Organized Improvement." Kaizen involves the development of action plans that "preplan" improvements. This effort results in a system that continuously improves all processes in a company. In other words, as a company forecasts its budget every year, a Kaizen-developed company will forecast its improvements or innovations in advance.

The CSI workbook draws from many of TQM's and Kaizen's processes and approaches that have allowed other companies to improve their performance. Because the Workbook is designed for an early stage team formation, in-depth discussions of quality concepts, such as Statistical Process Control (SPC) or other high level team concepts are overviewed only.

The CSI workbook is outlined to allow a facilitator to teach the process over 14-16 sessions (and weeks), sometimes one hour each week during that time, and for others, three times weekly. The challenge of a shorter period is the rate of understanding of the participants, and in the event that they are not able to do their homework or do miss a class, due to business requirements. We suggest at least a twelve

week period to create consistency while institutionalizing the individual's time for team work or personal development.

Finally, there is always a fear of change and doing things in a different way. Those who have been able to succeed within the current management system may not want to try something new. People who are either flexible or have been stifled by the current management system may embrace the team process at a faster pace than others in order to see new or better results.

Please be mindful that as you begin this journey down the "river of no return" into team management systems, we need to have everyone on board. Few people can run the four minute mile; therefore, our focus is not on the speed of the race. Our desire is for the entire group to cross the finish line, because everyone wins, and no one loses. We sometimes find people who may not see the need for teams or do not understand the process. Encourage them to visit with either their supervisor or the team facilitator if it appears that their resistance is slowing down the business-wide process.

The CSI Workbook chapters are broken down into three developmental processes:

Teams & Innovation Skills
    1) Creating a Team System
    2) Team Decision Skills
    3) problem stat Process, Part 1
    4) Problem Solving, Part 2

Working with a Team Process
    5) Customer Requirements
    6) Measurements & Scorecards
    7) Implementing Change

Fundamental Concepts
    8) The Business Life Cycle
    9) Management Concepts
    10) Management Process Concepts
    11) Personal Development
    12) Getting Results

As you begin this process of forming High Performance Teams, the leadership of your company has committed to having this system work. Innovation will die without it. New teams will learn that the way decisions are made, the way information is shared, and the pain that goes with poor execution must change. Your company's leadership is depending on YOU to learn new ways of thinking and working. That is the beginning of Innovation.

Your leaders may be "forced" to ask you to complete the CSI workbook because their (or your) customers are demanding cheaper prices, faster deliveries, improved quality, and fewer mistakes in the sales quote/order or manufacturing process. It may be that competitive threats are looming; and, although you do not know it, your leaders do. The Internet is changing the way business is operating. Team processes have a way to improve operational performance and employee satisfaction.

Whatever the reason your company has chosen this path towards empowered teams, building teams is not a recent fad. Team formation is a proven, successful method of empowering people to solve problems effectively, improve the organization's culture, and to create the foundation for a growing profitable company through innovation.

Your company's investment in money, time, and resources for YOU will have very little impact without YOUR contribution. Doing the homework, attending the classes, participating in team meetings, and all the other things involved may not excite everyone. We hope you will give the CSI method your best effort.

Our desire is to help build a system that improves your company's ability to remain competitive, with satisfied customers, competitively priced products and new products, a stable and performing work force with new skills and competencies, and profits to reinvest back into the business.

Organizations are now losing technical and organizational experience to retirement and outsourcing. Boards and Shareholders are now valuing their organizations by their ability to develop leadership or Gene pools of competent leaders, not just managers. Companies are also discovering that leadership must have multifunctional experience with risk taking success and failure. These needs are not easy to fulfill. We use this book as an integral part of a succession planning process that also includes our facilitated annual retreats. Over the years, we have performed this retreat/ team building process on hundreds of organizations, with dramatic results. In all cases, the companies have seen profitable growth. While we have been insultants to some of the staff of the organization (see chapter 8 on Life Cycles) many others have identified with this workbook's approach, and reaped great value for themselves and their company.

One other note about this book. The redesign was prompted by a client of ours, who expressed that while the content was informative, the design was "lousy and unprofessional". Their words did hurt, but their message was *so* clear. This new workbook design is intended to help *you* improve your success from the use of this workbook. Of note, we have added more outside margins to the pages, so you could add notes for later review. We also made it easier for the internal trainers we develop to follow through with their approach during our "train the trainer" sessions.

The Key to implementation is working off of a leadership retreat that identifies the top 10 opportunities and threats. With 10 action plans pasted to a wall, attendees vote the top 3-5 to begin each action plan's Forming stage after a few weeks to set things up. From those voted 3-5 action plans, leaders and members are selected and assigned to a sponsor. We then select another person to begin leading the classroom training, and schedule out the weekly class schedule, meeting 1 hour, 2 times a week for 15 weeks. The purpose of 2 meetings a week is to allow those who can't meet one day, can meet the other day. Once the schedule is in place, the action planning teams will meet the week after the first class. Sometimes, it is best to wait 4-6 weeks before forming, to allow the teams to be trained on the problem-solving techniques. After the Action Planning Team's first week, future dates are scheduled going out 15 weeks, just to be sure enough time was allocated for finish. Once the team is finished, either a new team is formed from the next available action plan, or spinoffs from the original team are formed.

As a final remark, we have learned that the CSI learning process will require three years of commitment to see positive results.

- The first year is for education and experimentation.

- The second year requires the active use of action planning and developing clearer scorecards.

- By the third year, most of the bugs are worked out and the organization is now performing at a much higher level.

- In each of the 3 years, we always recommend that our clients invest in our 2-day annual leadership retreat to identify the top 10 problems that teams can come together for and attack those problems. Just forming teams without key problems to solve will not improve performance.

- After 3 years, your organization should have discovered new leaders to build your company"s gene pool of talent, as well as develop the cross functional experience that reduces the silo affect that so many companies are struggling with.

CHAPTER 1
CREATING
A TEAM SYSTEM

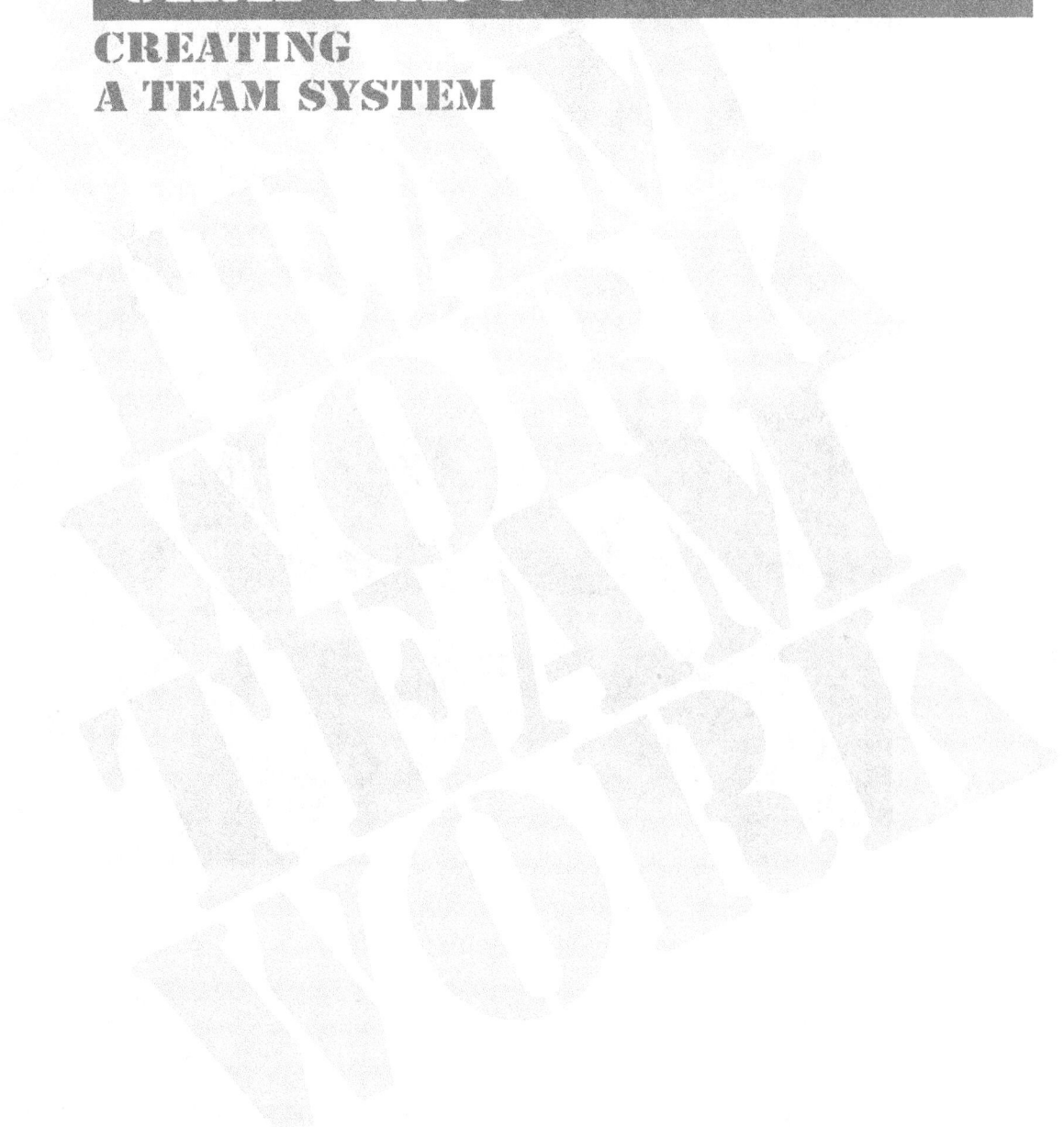

CREATING A TEAM SYSTEM

Team-Based Organizations

Team-Based Organizations have several characteristics relating to performance and learning. The most common aspects are:

1) Teams are formed to manage and/or improve performance.

2) Teams are used to share knowledge and experience among the members to produce well thought out decisions and strategies.

3) Everyone is involved with teams. However, in the early stages of team formation, the management team develops its processes first, and then the team process permeates throughout the remainder of the organization.

4) Teams are not built to create a new management structure for senior level managers to redirect the company from above. Teams are used to innovate the company from the bottom up. As a result, management can focus on strategic rather than operational issues.

5) Once the team system is in place, it becomes a permanent part of the organization, requiring 100% participation.

Four Primary Stakeholders

Leadership Team: The function of the leadership team is to develop and define Mission Vision Values of the company, to define successful outcomes of performance, and finally to Plan, Support, and Provide accountability to the teams with evaluation and feedback/reinforcement.

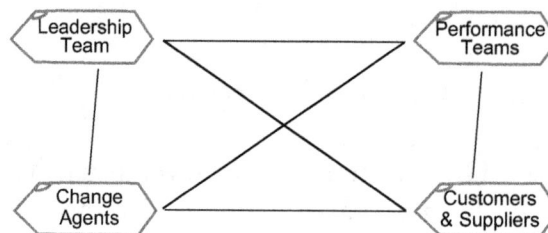

High Performance Team: A High Performance Team defines the team's primary issues and action plans to produce results. Performance teams are required to manage themselves and their implementation processes by defining a customer's requirements, developing measurements or scorecards to define success, and diagnosing and solving problems.

Change Agents: People or groups of people whose primary role is to develop a project plan with a team, educate or be educated by the team, and to implement those plans as the primary project leader. These people are either internal or external consultants.

Customers & Suppliers: People or groups of people who provide the team with the input or define the outputs that a team needs to improve performance. Customers or Suppliers could be other teams, other divisions, lower level employees, the traditional external customers who pay the invoices a company creates, or the vendor/supplier a company buys products or services from.

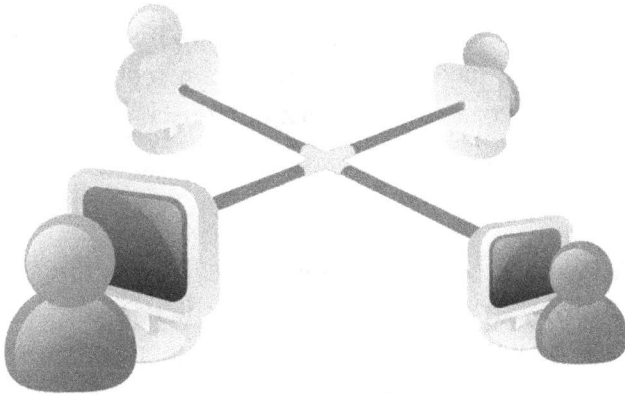

What are the benefits of having Teams?

Teams are forums for communication, as well as being an educational, knowledge sharing tool. Teams are also used to develop leadership from below, by introducing to leadership candidates the opportunity to work with other functional areas, develop internal networks for support, and to improve their capacity to develop others as well. Therefore, information should be passed throughout the team on a regular basis, and meetings held regularly to facilitate the process.

Once successfully implemented, teams provide an ongoing sense of community and camaraderie. They also provide support to each participant as each team member shares their insights for solving problems or issues.

Teams produce results. The primary purpose of teams is to improve process performance in four areas: *Creativity*, *Quality*, *Cycle Times*, and *Costs*.

Creativity, or *innovation*, is the process of developing new products or services, creating new ways of doing things, or creating better products or services to provide to a customer. The Key words are "New" and "Better."

Quality, as defined by Dr. W. Edwards Deming, is "Pride in Workmanship." Quality represents the anticipation, conforming to, or exceeding of a customer's requirements. Dr. Deming developed fourteen points to his management methods and we have consolidated them to the following six. We will be covering his work in later chapters.

TEAM TIP

Institute a vigorous program of education, training, and retraining.

A summary of the list is:

1) **Adopt a new Philosophy**—Quality—as the company's religion. Then, align the company's purpose with Continuous Improvement of Product and Services Innovation & Change. Create Systems that support Continuous Improvement.

2) **End dependence on Mass Inspection** and end the Practice of awarding business on Price Tag alone.

3) Institute a vigorous program of **education, training, and retraining**.

4) **Institute leadership** by accepting personal failure for a subordinate's failure, and drive out fear of retribution when things go wrong.

5) **Break down barriers between staff areas**, as well as barriers to pride of workmanship. Properly formed teams should be "cross functional" to remove staff barriers.

6) **Eliminate targets, quotas, and slogans** for the workforce, but provide information and systems that will enable the workforce to change or improve over time.

The term "Cycle Time" represents the measurement from the input into the process to the output to the customer. What should be noted is that the longer the cycle time is, the less responsive the process is to the customer's needs, because it actually translates to a higher cost.

TEAMWO K

Costs, as described by Eli Goldratt in his book, *The Goal*, are "all the money the system spends in order to turn inventory into throughput." There are only three ways to reduce costs of a system without injuring the customer or company: **Change procedures** that reduce cycle time and handling; implement **training** and retraining to improve rework and mistakes; and implement **robotics**, or technology that reduces or eliminates human interference within the system.

Team Formation

Enabling a Team-Based system in an organization takes time. Management has to develop trust that the teams will perform well, and avoid creating "gridlock" in the decision-making process. In today's fast-paced working environment, the ability to respond quickly to change encumbers teams to meet regularly to educate and implement changes. There are three basic types of teams that evolve over time: **Functional Teams, Cross-Functional Teams, and Multifunctional Teams**.

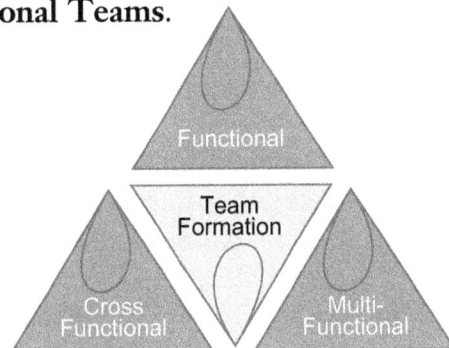

> **definition**
>
> *Team Formations:* There are three basic types of teams that evolve over time: **Functional Teams, Cross-Functional Teams, and Multifunctional Teams.**

Functional Teams:

Functional Teams are comprised of groups of similar skills and expertise. For example, there are Sales Teams, Finance Teams, Operations Teams, and Administrative or Customer Service Teams. Their focus usually involves micro management issues, such as work center changes or specific task implementation.

Cross-Functional Teams:

Cross-Functional teams are those individuals who are grouped together by the differences in their disciplines. They usually represent, as individuals, their respective functional teams to provide a wider view of issues and solutions to problems. These teams are usually involved in company wide change or project implementation.

Multifunctional Teams:

Multifunctional Team members are usually competent in several disciplines or are in leadership positions. The advantage to these teams is that they are far more flexible and responsive to customer needs. As a result, their ability to understand most, if not all, aspects of the business allows for orderly change. In many cases, the leadership team represents many of the various functional and cross functional teams in order to create positive change.

Results-Oriented Teams: Ten Critical Success Factors

1) **Systems Alignment:** Over the years of implementation, the entire company's approach toward change will involve all facets and practices of the business. Nothing is sacred.

2) **Customer Focused:** Change must be driven by customer needs, not internal needs. It is by satisfying customers that positive changes evolve.

3) **Team Score Keeping:** All teams will be driven by a "Balanced Scorecard." That is, measurements reflect the customer's desired results from a customer satisfaction, financial, and business perspective.

4) **Continuous Improvement:** This process is about small incremental changes throughout the organization, or the elimination of unneeded steps, activities, or processes. It is about changing habits and developing creativity.

5) **100% Participation:** After the initial stages are implemented, further team development into the lower ranks will achieve higher yields. A company's ability to move quickly in a fast-paced environment requires a flatter organization with highly trained and educated people, developed through teams.

6) **Internal Coaches:** The challenge in every organization over the next 15 years is the depletion of experience, as seasoned people head for retirement. In addition, the company's ability to develop and retrain individuals will require coaching and mentoring. Teams provide a sensible approach to developing the next generation of managers and leaders.

7) **Flatter Management Layers:** A team-based company does not require layers of middle managers to control information flow. Teams will be built around key processes and will make the decisions regarding their performance.

8) **Driven by Line Management**: This means that teams will be practiced by line management, as they will be responsible for creating teams, being held accountable for their teams' success and rewarding only those who participate.

TEAM TIP

Change must be driven by customer needs, not internal needs. It is by satisfying customers that positive changes evolve.

9) **Results Based**: Eli Goldratt's *The Goal* clarified that "the goal" was to make money. Objectives must have understandable business results. Performance based on confusing or conflicting goals will result in bureaucracy or unneeded internal conflicts.

10) **Rewards & Recognition**: This is the final topic for a very good reason. You cannot reward and recognize until you have achieved the nine success factors. Not only does a company need to change quickly, but people want swifter responses for good performance. This topic will be discussed further in chapters 7 and 10.

Team Activities: The Step by Step Process for Continuous Improvement

The early formation of teams is usually an awkward time for all participants. The success of team implementation requires a formalized process of problem solving. The following steps are a guideline for early success and training using teams. We use the terms Forming, Storming, Norming, and Performing.

FORMING: Institute the team by establishing regular and consistent times and places for the meetings. Establish the purpose and direction of the team, including ground rules and communication systems, (i.e., memos, email, phone).

STORMING: In this stage, the key is identifying customers and their needs, products and services required, and the team's role and responsibility. Then it requires interviews with the customers and suppliers to identify key processes requiring change. This stage, also known as "Brain Storming," is where innovation, creativity, and new ideas come to the surface.

NORMING: Norming refers to the process of analyzing the team process (Process Mapping) after the storming stage is almost finished, identifying the key measurements involved in the process, and developing scorecards for both business performance and customer satisfaction. This process may include graphing, tracking, or creating goals.

PERFORMING: The final stage relates to the team's ability to problem solve. Problem solving refers to the process of identifying the real causes of the problem, analyzing the alternatives, implementing a new course of action, and evaluating the change as being positive or negative to the desired result. We will review this area in chapters 3 and 4.

Team Membership

The membership of a team is broken down into the following definitions:

Sponsor: The key or Senior Manager who is, or who reports to, the president. Sponsors must own the success of the team and who is its leader, from a managerial point of view. It is very common for teams to face resistance to change and ideas that the team will identify and want to implement. It is the Sponsor's duty and responsibility to actively support the team's efforts and to guide them through the difficulties of corporate politics and fiefdoms, which often destroys the team's effectiveness and commitment to change.

Team Leader: Depending on the organization, it is the manager or the manager's selected leader who is responsible for the output of the team. In most cases, we suggest selecting a non-manager, as this person will have opportunities to develop leadership skills while learning new things.

Team Member: the people who participate on the team and "own" the process. We sometimes suggest that one member be in management, so that the team has support to complete their mission/Tasks. Members are expected to participate and work for success. Members are selected by Management.

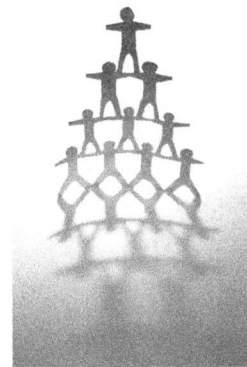

Team Coach or Consultant: The advisor who is not a member of the team, but who assists/advises in team implementation & research.

Experts: People who have acquired valuable knowledge or experience for the team to use, but are not "Team Members." We usually ask for the executive team or outside professionals to be considered for their input, or it could be any employee with technical knowledge, such as IT or Accounting.

Effective Team Meetings:

There are several areas that will significantly change the effectiveness of a team meeting. They include: developing basic ground rules, the meeting's environment, content, and agenda, and each member's communication skills. Effective team meetings are the result of good team leadership and membership skills.

BASIC GROUND RULES: The list below is just a sampling of items that would help make meetings productive and constructive:

TEAM TIP

Everyone has the responsibility to contribute, but the ideas belong to the group, not to the individual.

1) *One person talks at a time*, with no interruptions, no gossiping while a person speaks, and the speaker speaks for a limited period of time, say three to five minutes.

2) *Arrive on time and end on time.*

3) *Stick to the topic at hand;* discuss other issues after the current topic has been addressed.

4) *Be a good listener;* ask questions when appropriate.

5) *Be clear, frank and honest, but without malice or value judgments.* Avoid criticism of a person or personal remarks that would cause harm or create a negative atmosphere. One of Deming's favorite remarks is

"85% of the problems are caused by the system, not people." The team approach is to correct the system.

6) *Everyone has the responsibility to contribute*, but the ideas belong to the group, not to the individual.

7) The team leader's responsibility is to *encourage participation*, not to dominate the conversation.

Planning the Meeting involves where the meeting takes place, what topics are to be covered, and a written agenda to keep the meeting on track. We have found it to be very difficult to get people to show up when there is a lack of structure and routine. We also find it hard to get people from different departments to work together because their managers want them to also get work done.

WHERE: A consistent time and place creates habits and are a part of the normal business routine. Booking a room that will allow for few interruptions or distractions, good seating, and a properly maintained temperature, can usually be found anywhere. Equipment, such as chalk boards, presentation projectors and screens, as well as flip charts and easels with writing utensils may also be important.

WHEN: Much like TV shows, meetings should be scheduled regularly, usually weekly for about an hour. In the early stages, the time is spent "getting a feel" for interacting as a team. As time moves on, the challenges will be on communicating with each member about changes that take place and solutions to problems. It has been found that early morning meetings are best for participation and contribution.

Other suggestions for meetings are:
Daily: for 10-20 minutes
Weekly: 30-60 minutes
Biweekly: 1-2 hours
Monthly: 4-8 hours

> **TEAM TIP**
>
> *There are primarily three parts to the agenda:* **Planning, Managing, and Follow-up.**

DEVELOPING AN AGENDA:

There are primarily three parts to the agenda: **Planning, Managing, and Follow-up**. The Planning Stage involves the following steps:

❏ Review prior meetings "minutes" and related topics.

❏ Prioritize unfinished business and new business.

❏ Send out agendas in advance, sometimes posting this document to a bulletin board.

❏ Ask team members for input.

❏ Make the agenda visible during meeting.

Managing the agenda can be difficult at times, due to the topic involved or the members' interest in the topic. As the meeting unfolds, some suggested ways to keep the meeting productive are as follows:

❏ Review the agenda at the beginning, setting time limits if necessary.

❏ Share information regarding changes or concerns that may involve the team.

❏ Review the team performance.

❏ Review progress with current action plans to ensure meeting of expected timelines or benchmarks.

❏ Recognize team members for their positive contribution or performance.

❏ Problem solving may be involved and could consume most of the time in the early stages of a team. Such time should be anticipated and allotted

TEAM TIP

Functional Teams, such as the sales team, should rotate their leaders every quarter or semi-annually to give others a chance to lead the team. It should not be run by the manager.

Cross Functional Teams, such as a problem solving team, should not change or rotate their leader because their project timelines usually require one leader to finish the project.

so that people have a chance to participate and contribute.

❑ Developing action plans evolves as a result of the team making a decision from the problem solving area and requires an implementation schedule or action plan to monitor and review.

❑ All meetings should close with a summary from the meeting to be written up as minutes; selecting the person who will be responsible for writing up the next agenda and taking minutes should be made, and an agreement to the next meeting's time and place. If team leaders rotate on a regular basis, those leader issues should be addressed before closing.

IF A VOTE IS REQUIRED:

There are times in a meeting when the members must come to a decision by vote. This is sometimes called consensus. And it usually involves some problem that cannot be enacted without others' agreement or "buy-in". Here are some suggestions to create effective team decisions in the event it is required:

1. Define the criteria for the BEST solution.

2. If there is a list of ideas or solutions, CULL (or trim) the list first. Get the best solutions on a final list. Use a Pros and Cons approach, by identifying the strengths and weaknesses of each item.

3. Combine, if possible, the remaining items into reasonable groupings of solutions, so that a vote can be made on several issues, not just one.

4. Look at the new list, and discuss which group or item would make the biggest positive impact to the solution.

TEAM TIP

Minutes Best Practices

• *To improve writing skills, rotate the minutes taker so one person does not always take the minutes*

• *Final minutes should include next meeting's agenda*

• *Once minutes are prepared, send out to members for correction or discussion before next meeting*

• *Once minutes are approved, post in prominent location to share team's progress with others*

5. Ask the members if they have any further viable solutions to add to the discussion. The reason you ask for other viable solutions is that new ideas may develop that should be shared. Be mindful, most of the best ideas are developed at the *end* of a meeting, not at the beginning.

6. Once the information has been presented and a vote has been made, ask each member if they will support the decision. This will help identify any resistance to the plan, and allows a final expression of commitment by the members to the final approach.

TEAM MEETING AGENDA

Item#	Agenda Item	Time Frame
A	Review the Agenda	
B	Review Team's Performance	
C	Review Current Action Plans	
D	Recognize Team Members	
E	Problem Solving Session	
F	Action Planning for New Projects	
G	Plan Next Team Meeting	

Meeting Results   Date

Members Attended	Decisions Made:

Team Meeting Checklist

This checklist below reminds the team leader and the membership of any items forgotten or left out from the preparation process:

Done?	Agenda item
☐	What needs to be finished at this meeting?
☐	Is the location and time set?
☐	For long meetings, have breaks been added?
☐	Is the agenda sent out in advance of mtg?
☐	Are the agenda topics prioritized?
☐	What activities should be done?
☐	What information are you missing?
☐	Are there set time limits?
☐	Did you allow new items to the agenda?
☐	Do you have the right people attending?
☐	How will you insure participation?
☐	Does each member know what to bring?
☐	Do you have enough people to have a mtg?
☐	Is the person doing the minutes showing up?
☐	Are the refreshments arranged?
☐	Do you have all your presentation equipment?
☐	Are all the measurements done correctly?

CHAPTER 2

BUILDING TEAM
DECISION SKILLS

Learning Objective Questions from Chapter One: Creating a Team Situation

✎ Who are the four Primary Stakeholders?

✎ What is the difference between a functional team and a cross-functional team?

✎ What is the difference between a cross-functional team and a multi-functional team?

✎ Describe the four types of team member roles.

✎ If your team is going to meet on a weekly basis, what is the suggested length of time to meet?

BUILDING TEAM DECISION SKILLS

Introduction

Team decisions are a function of the team members desiring better results, converging with the collection and analysis information relating to the issues that are harming the results. In the previous chapter, we reviewed the patterns of team formation, the steps involved in effective team formation, and how to manage time while working in teams. We are now going to review the decision-making process viewed by several different authors.

Evolution of Team Decision-Making Styles

Peter Drucker's first book on management, *The Practice of Management*, describes how teams should work. He illustrates a doubles tennis team, two people who have built trust with each other, and have learned to cover for each other. The more they play together, the more often they see a final result... to win. Unlike their years of individual play, these tennis players have learned that each must volley a serve while the other stands back and prepares for the opponents' return volley. They learn to work together effectively in order to win.

As we look at the doubles team, we can gather insights to management teams. They both have members with complementary and different skills. One person may be a more dominant player in one area, such as service than the other.

We have found that the best singles players usually do not play well in doubles tournaments. It is difficult to read—just a singles player's mindset of singlehandedly taking care of all volleys to begin trusting their partner to finish the play. The individual dynamics and team dynamics for both the tennis player and the management team member play an integral part in the team's culture. "Lone Rangers", or people who like to work alone, have difficult times working in teams. Every organization has "Lone Rangers" and it is very important that the team system accepts them just as they must accept working with others.

Therefore, it is very important that team members recognize their strengths and weaknesses, both as individuals

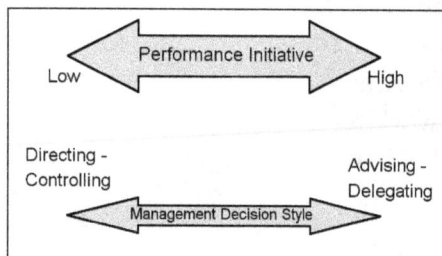

and as a team. We will be discussing individual decision-making styles later in this chapter. At this point, we need to understand the *team* dynamics, and its evolution in decision-making styles.

The functioning of a team is influenced by the performance initiatives of the individuals in conjunction with the individuals' decision-making styles.

As a team builds trust, the members increase their ability to "let go" of control, and to allow the team to help them make better decisions. As the members see positive results from teams, due to having support and help from their teammates, their performance initiative rises. Over time, the ideal team grows from a tentative, developing performance behavior to a high-energy, fastpaced, highly competent and performing management team.

	Controlling Directing	Advising Delegating
	(Over Control)	(High Performance teams)
High	High Energy Misdirected Performance	High Energy Competence Performance
Low	Low Trust Competence Performance	Low Energy Performance
	(Parental Style)	(Premature Empowerment)

Source: Lawrence Miller and Jennifer Howard

Teams don't always work. In the "Over Control" section of the diagram, controlling managers or rebellious teams surface as a lack of training, or unclear responsibility builds an atmosphere where discouragement emerges. As a result, anger, hostility, or apathy toward change rises. Often, people are blamed and heads roll.

Premature Empowerment (PE) occurs when management defers *too much* responsibility, too little direction, and not enough feedback to encourage the teams to grow. When "PE" occurs, management becomes too permissive, and team satisfaction comes from the quality of work life, not business or operating performance. Self management of the team, and the lack of accountability of management to help the teams go forward creates an atmosphere of frustration and skepticism.

> **definition**
>
> ***Premature Empowerment*** (PE) occurs when management defers *too much* responsibility, too little direction, and not enough feedback to encourage the teams to grow.

The key to successful team development is the personal pursuit of knowledge and technical skills, focusing on needs and requirements of the customer, and developing problem-solving abilities. Management needs to improve their coaching and teaching skills, and enable system and structure changes that will empower when performance is measured and self-maintained by the teams.

Organizational Cultural Roles: Ichak Adizes

Ichak Adizes researched and identified consistent organizational patterns that influence a company's performance. These cultural patterns are described in four words: Production, Administration, Entrepreneurism, and Integration.

Production or Producer relates to team members who focus on results predictably and reliably. A "Producer" develops clear measurements of success and focuses attention on getting those results. Producers "love" action, and lots of it. They are the people who clearly help grow the business by their strong focus on action for results.

Administration or Administrators are members that do not look for things getting done, but "how" they get done. They are constantly fighting with producers to do things right the first time, because it is more efficient to do so. Administrators desire control, so that the mistakes producers make are not repeated. Conflicts rise when the new "Controller" comes in, implementing new rules or "controls" to keep the company growing, with profits. Producers don't always see that.

Entrepreneur stands for the team's ability to create new things or innovate by making things better. Unlike a producer and administrator, entrepreneurship is a long-term developing style. It is very easy to create new sales effort or system controls. What's *not* easy is encouraging and developing new ideas that will create new products and services the customer requires or desires at a reasonable cost. One of the best ways to enable entrepreneurship is with leadership styles that do not condemn failure, but enable growth to come from failure. The most common phrase for an entrepreneurial team is "It is permitted, unless forbidden."

Integration relates to the team's ethics and core values. It is about how people "integrate" with each other, working together with friendliness and trust. Integration is also a long-term developmental process because it is very hard to build trust once it is lost. It is very hard to make people like each other when they have had hardships with each other. In many cases, integration becomes a problem when the mantra is: "don't rock the boat, we have always done it this way successfully."

Individual Decision-Making Styles

Now that we have covered group dynamics and cultural roles, we now focus our attention on your personal decision-making styles. Regardless of how your team is developed or grouped, each individual's decision-making style will influence the team's decision-making process. There are four well known management decision-making styles: **Delegation, Command, Consultive, and Consensus.**

Delegation style means that a person has been given authority to decide on his/her own, without prior approval. For example, if you tell a Senior in High School to "go to the store and buy some fruit" with the money you just gave, then you are delegating the following decisions: How to get there, what store to use, what fruit to pick, and how much to pay. You did not control their choices if they paid for a cab, drove your car, rode their bike, or asked a friend to drive. There is always an issue about a change, if any occurred.

The challenge in delegation is that if a person does not have the correct or timely information, he/she may not make a correct decision. Communication is very important with delegation. In addition, if the person makes a decision that affects other parts of the business, then more problems will arise. Therefore, training and cross-training are key processes required for successful delegation.

> **definition**
>
> **Delegation style:** means that a person has been given authority to decide on his/her own, without prior approval.

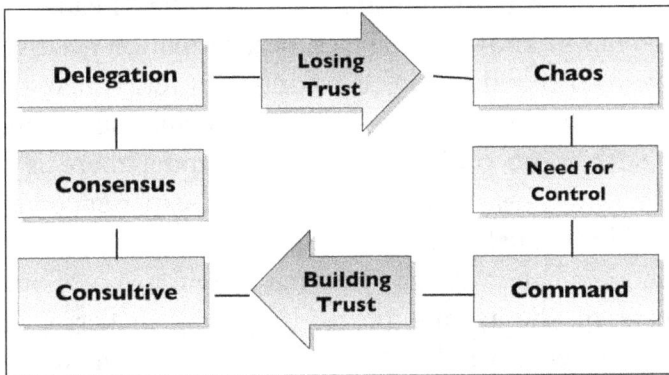

```
Delegation ── Losing      ─  Chaos
                Trust
    │                          │
Consensus                 Need for
                          Control
    │                          │
Consultive ── Building   ─  Command
                Trust
```

The fundamental concern with delegation is that trust be developed. Trusting your child to make the right decisions, and return all the change, means he/she will have learned your needs and expectations, and will have been trained to deliver those needs without much communication. As such, delegation takes a very long time to develop correctly. It requires patience and follow-through.

One challenge with team development processes is to build as much delegation as possible, without creating command-style structures. By flattening an organizational structure without training and information support, chaos occurs. As chaos, or random actions of errors and mistakes develop, trust is broken. At this point, a person's ability to rebuild trust forces leaders of the organization to regain control. Where delegation is the lack of detail control, command is at the opposite side of the spectrum.

Command style refers to a decision made by an individual without conferring with others. This type of style works great under crisis, when decisions are made quickly and results show up just as fast. An example of the command style is the directive style of a police officer at the scene of an emergency. He/she will make decisions based on what they see at the time, without consulting other officers, or their supervisors. Their continuous training for various scenarios allows us to trust them to make the right decisions most of the time.

The downside of the command style involves several issues. The first is the presumption that the "Leader" or decision maker knows all the facts or information necessary to make a correct decision. Working with teams may take more time to discuss issues, but the information is much richer with more options. In a crisis mode, there is no time to confer, just to act. That is where experienced and seasoned individuals bring value quickly.

Another issue with the command style involves other members of the team—the non-decision makers—who may not agree with the decision. Without contribution or participation of others, commitment is at risk. As a

definition

Command style: decisions made without conferring with others. Works well under crisis, but other members of team may not agree or follow-through, leading to a situation viewed as being unsuccessful after implementation.

result, lack of follow-through by key individuals may make the decision appear appropriate at the time; but it will be viewed as unsuccessful after implementation, due to a lack of follow-through by those needed to perform well.

Consultive style is the next stage of team development, and refers to the process of involving others in the decision, but only with *advice*. The consultive style is the most commonly used, because most day-to-day decisions do not have crisis constraints, nor do they influence other departments significantly. Therefore, it is a quick and flexible process for gathering information before a decision is made. It also begins the process of inviting other people into the decision-making process. However, if a person's advice is not taken, the decision maker risks alienating the advisor, or at best, decreasing the advisor's willingness for future involvement.

Consensus style refers to those decisions that are very complex, or have a significant impact on several stakeholder groups. As a result, it is used for less than 15% of all decisions. In most cases, these decisions involve strategic issues, requiring in-depth analysis and requiring more "buy-in" or commitment/ownership for successful implementation. With more people involved, an increased commitment and improved quality of the decision evolves.

However, consensus is not about getting 100% of the votes. It is about agreeing to the best solution, without "finger-pointing" at a person if things fail. Weaknesses to the consensus style usually show up as a lack of decision making, when no one can agree to a decision, or the group members are incapable of making a decision.

Also, consensus style tends to develop a lack of accountability within management. We promote the understanding that if a team cannot make a decision, then the leadership must make it for them. As a result, there will be times when a team may fluctuate between consensus and consulting, depending on the nature of the decision as well as the abilities of the members to vote and then act upon a decision.

definition

Consensus style: used for less than 15% of all decisions, typically involves strategic issues, requires in-depth analysis, requires more 'buy-in' or commitment/ownership for successful implementation—can lead to an increased commitment and improved quality decision.

39

Consensus will most likely occur when the following conditions occur:

- ✔ There is a genuine purpose to seek new, creative or innovative solutions, with agreed upon criteria before the solution is selected.

- ✔ There is a common goal, with common understanding of the problem.
- ✔ All information is equally shared, searching for systemic causes, not people that result in the problem.

- ✔ All views are honestly shared, and were considered with respect and without interruption and prejudice.

- ✔ Members are flexible and are willing to listen to opposing arguments, are willing to support the group's decision as if it was their own, and are willing to put aside their own position for the teams'.

One of the challenges in developing teams over time is the integration of "Lone Rangers" or people who tend to work on their own, resisting outside intervention or sharing of information. We have learned over the years that the "Lone Rangers" of the world get things done, but rarely effectively if they do not develop team skills to get others to help them. How about the person who is known to be "crabby" because they work so hard, but won't let anyone help them. How about the person who has all the knowledge, works hard, but can't get things finished because there are too many "fires" burning. What about the person who is a hard worker, but who is complaining constantly about something yet can't seem to get their act together with others.

If you notice, the words "hard worker," and "knowledgeable," are merged with "unfinished" and "unhappy." Lone rangers lose their effectiveness over time due to many factors.

Homework Assignment

Please write down situations that you believe illustrate the proper use for each of the four decision-making styles: Delegation, Consensus, Consultive, and Command. For example, under Delegation, "Ordering cleaning supplies, inputting invoices" ; under Consensus, "New product strategies".

Delegation:

Consensus:

Consultive:

Command:

CHAPTER 3

DEVELOPING PROBLEM SOLVING SKILLS
PART1: FORMING & STORMING

Learning Objective Questions from
Chapter Two: Building Team Decision Skills

✎ *What are the four Cultural Roles by Ichak Adizes?*

✎ *What are the four Decision-Making Styles?*

DEVELOPING PROBLEM SOLVING SKILLS

PART 1: FORMING & STORMING

Problem Solving as a Strategy

One of the fundamental laws of thermodynamics is that anything that does not move or remains in an unchanging state will gradually deteriorate. Just leave a car parked on the side of a highway for a month or two and the environment around it will gradually take its toll. Rust will develop, thieves may take the tires, the paint will be scratched by the sandblasting of passing cars, and so forth. A company that does not learn to solve problems effectively will be as subject to its environment as the parked car.

Gerry Faust, Dick Lyles, and Will Phillips wrote in their book, *Responsible Managers get Results* that there are three basic categories of problems: People, Operational, and Technical. People problems are primarily behavioral issues. Technical problems involve mechanical, electronic, or equipment systems failures. Operational problems, however, involve everything else, such as marketplace dynamics, functional specialties, such as marketing or finance, and/or organizational structure issues.

We have developed an eight-step method for problem solving using teams:

1) Define the Problem
2) Define the Objective(s)
3) Analyze the Possible Causes
4) Generate Alternative Solutions
5) Develop an Action Plan
6) Communicate to those involved
7) Pilot a Solution Troubleshoot
8) Monitor and Follow-up while Implementing

Identifying the Problem

In Peter Senge's book, *The Fifth Discipline*, there are Eleven Laws of Systems Thinking (the Fifth Discipline) of a "Learning Organization." When identifying a problem, the easiest, most obvious causes of the problem are usually not the "real" cause of the problem.

Our approach to problem solving is to help companies develop the ability to define and analyze a problem correctly by finding the "real" root causes, rather than the surface issues. Senge's Laws of System Thinking helps put the identity issues in true perspective, so that higher level problem solving can take place.

As an example, if a light bulb in the office is out, the easiest solution is to replace it. When you find yourself replacing the bulb in one socket as well as others every day, then problem solving takes a new turn. We suggest you think of the light bulb example when you read through the laws.

The Eleven laws are:

1) **"Today's problems come from yesterday's solutions,"** meaning that if you solve a problem in one area of the system today, another system will unknowingly be affected later. *I wonder if the electrician messed around with the lights when he was in yesterday?*

2) **"The harder you push, the harder the system pushes back,"** refers to 'Compensating Feedback' or the reaction by a system to an operational change occurring elsewhere. It is similar to the old adage "For every action there is a reaction." *Was that light switch for the new office next door installed properly?*

3) **"Behavior grows better before it grows worse,"** means that there is a time delay before reality sinks in and reactions to change take place. *We have now changed bulbs every day for the last week, what is happening here?*

4) **"The easy way out usually leads back in,"** that is, familiar stories, or continually following what we know best, may not solve the problem. *Maybe we bought a bad batch of light bulbs. Let's change the vendor.*

5) **"The cure could be worse than the disease,"** relates to the effect of implementing an easy solution only to find that the results are disastrous. *Now that we changed the light bulb vendor, we no longer get the discounts on electrical repair items.*

6) **"Faster is slower,"** relates to the organization's ability to accept change. When change comes too quickly, or is too complex, the body naturally slows down. *People are calling in sick or complaining. These new light bulbs from the new vendor may be causing eye problems.*

7) **Cause and effect are not closely related to "time and space,"** which refers to the concept that problems do not necessarily remain in the same area. For example, a costing problem may not be a manufacturing or an accounting problem, but a data input problem left unnoticed by another less obvious department. *Was that new power source for the new machine in the factory installed properly? Are we getting power spikes from it to affect our lights?*

8) **"Small changes can produce big results, but the areas of highest leverage are often less obvious,"** meaning that in some cases a minimal change may have a lasting, more optimal result than a very big change. For example: a small rudder will suffice for a very large ocean liner. *Can we borrow a volt-meter to monitor the power fluctuations?*

9) **"You can have your cake and eat it too, but not all at once,"** refers to the concept that it's not always true that you can't have something without sacrificing elsewhere. This law states that you can achieve

change and positive results over time, and that looking for instant results is fleeting. *Since we replaced the new power breaker—it was improperly installed—we have found that the new breaker actually handles even more outlets than planned.*

10) **"Dividing an elephant in half will not produce two small elephants,"** meaning that system boundaries are intertwined, and that to look at one part of the system without looking at the other parts is like fixing half an elephant. *Our installing a separate power line into our office to handle the light bulb issue has fixed our problem, but we still haven't fixed the shop's light problem.*

11) **"There is no blame,"** simply means that blaming others is not a solution, it may be part of the problem. *Why can't the mechanic install light bulbs correctly? This kind of stuff happens all the time!*

Senge also wrote of the process of "Dynamic Complexity." He related it to the process of filling a glass of water. The problem was to fill the glass from a faucet, to the desired mark on the glass. The problem could be solved by filling it to the top, and then emptying it to the mark; or, by filling it, then slowing the faucet at just the right moment, so that the water draining from the faucet arm fills the glass to the mark. In each case, you either sacrifice water for speed, or speed for water. A team's awareness of these types of issues increases the company's ability to solve very complex problems.

In summary, always accepting the easiest and most convenient solutions does not create long-term results. Be mindful that your implementation decisions have significant long-term effects, beyond the boundaries you may currently perceive.

Tools to Solve Problems

We have broken down some of the tools for problem solving into functional areas of the problem-solving stages. They can be used in other stages, but their primary use is in the following:

1) Define the Problem
   Pinpointing
2) Define the Objective(s)
   Pinpointing
3) Analyze the Possible Causes
   Data Gathering
   Cause & Effect Diagrams
   Pareto Charts
   Run Charts
4) Generate Alternative Solutions
   Brainstorming
   Consensus Reaching
5) Develop an Action Plan
6) Communicate to those involved
   Control Charts
   Gantt & Pert Charts
7) Pilot a Solution—Troubleshoot
   Brainstorming
8) Monitor and Follow-up while Implementing
   Run Charts
   Control Charts
   Gantt & Pert Charts

What is Pinpointing?

Pinpointing is the process of identifying the earliest cause of the problem. Defining a problem in the most detailed way helps to clarify what it is that you really want to solve. An airline company cannot solve the problem of late arrivals before it gets a clearer understanding of the issues that are causing the late arrival problems.

definition

Pinpointing: the process of identifying, in detail, the earliest cause of the problem.

For example, can the airline control late arrivals if there is a weather problem at the destination or departure airport? Should the airline modify or extend the scheduled arrival times to avoid having consistent delays? Does it matter which airports are involved? Does the type of aircraft matter? These pinpointing questions help define the problem further.

Pinpointing is about describing in clear detail the problem you wish to solve in a way that can easily be understood and then focused upon. Pinpointing may identify several problems within a bigger problem, and so it should, if the problem is either large in scope or complex. In many cases, pinpointing often creates several or very lengthy lists of problems from a "simple" problem statement.

Effective pinpointing requires a significant amount of hard data to help describe the problem. Good data helps define the objectives you will need to achieve once you have defined the problem. For example, instead of defining the problem as "late arrivals," it could be stated: "How do we improve our arrival rate in Chicago from 90% to 99%?" Or an even better problem statement would be: "How do we improve our arrival rate in Chicago from 88% to 99% for flights that are leaving the west coast, and that are arriving after 3 pm Chicago time?"

Analyzing the Data

Now that you have clearly defined the problem, and the problem statement sets the objectives to achieve, the real work begins. Collecting data should have started in the pinpointing stage, but a series of processes can be used to organize the data into meaningful patterns for analysis.

Cause and Effect Diagrams

Cause and effect diagrams are also known as "fishbone" diagrams, because they look like the backbones of fish. They are used to determine the root causes of a problem. As you review the diagram on the next page, you will see that we

Cause & Effect (Fishbone)

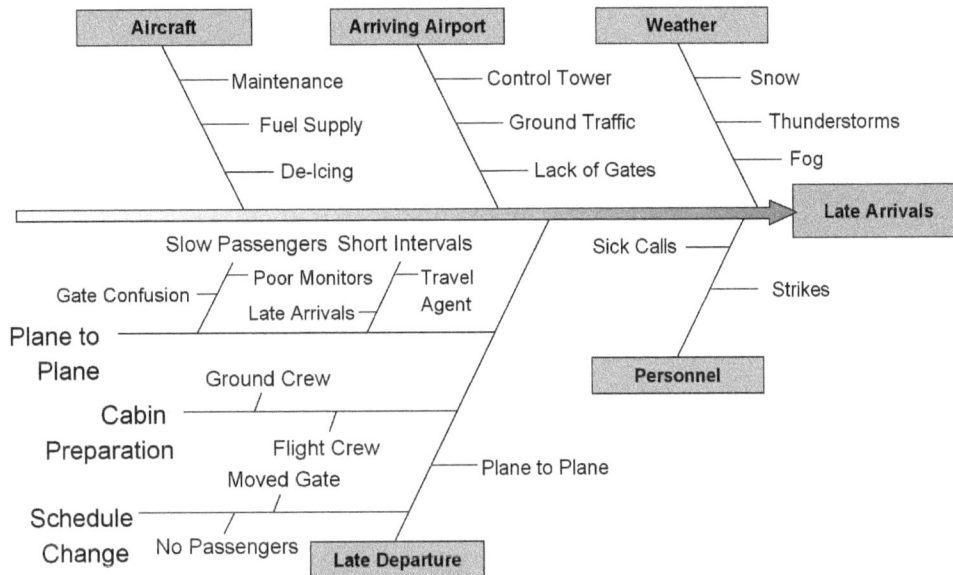

have outlined a few examples of how a fishbone is prepared, using the late aircraft scenario previously described.

The key is to describe the problem you are trying to solve, and to collect data that will help fill in the "fishbones."

The highlighted descriptions are the keys, main categories, or groupings for each cause.

By preparing the cause and effect diagram, you can see how complex the problem really is. Fixing it would require that several action plans be developed after a brainstorming session on each "bone" made. Some items, such as weather may be items outside of our control. Not allowing connecting flights at an airport without at least 45 minutes between flights could be a solution. As you can see, fixing delayed flights is not that simple.

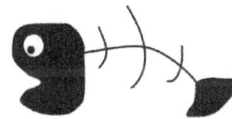

Pareto Charts

Pareto charts are illustrative bar charts that help determine which problems to solve *first*. An Italian economist, Vilfredo Pareto, developed the 80/20 rule that says 80% of the effects involve only 20% of the known set of causes. As an example, your team may discover that 80% of the late payments from customers are coming from 20% of the customer list. You may learn that 80% of the on-time delivery involves 20% of the product list. By using a Pareto Chart, we are organizing the issues in a way that allows us to solve 80% of the problems with 20% of the effort and time.

Building a Pareto Chart is a three-step process using an Excel or spreadsheet. In the following examples, the team collected late arrivals by *time of day* and placed this information in the spreadsheet as shown in the left column.

If the team were to graph the data at this point, the graph would look like the "Pareto Chart?" below:

	Late Arr's	Accum
8 AM	3	3
9 AM	6	6
10 AM	6	15
11 AM	3	18
12 AM	3	21
1 PM	5	26
2 PM	6	32
3 PM	7	39
4 PM	9	48
5 PM	8	56
6 PM	9	65
7 PM	10	75
8 PM	5	80
9 PM	4	84

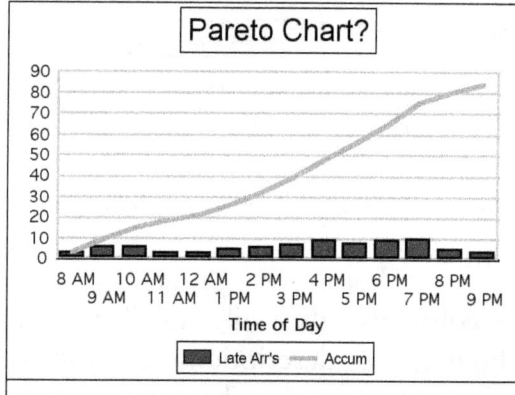

The next step is to rearrange the data with rankings by the highest and lowest in *frequency*, as shown below. To use the spreadsheet's ranking function, find the "@" functions in 1-2-3 or "Insert Function" in Excel and look under "**Rank**." From there, **sort** the Rank column and the other columns by RANK, using the sort function under "Data" or "Range."

After you have ranked and re-sorted the data, highlight the data, including the headings, and press the "Create Chart" icon, or the "Insert" or "Create" from the Task Bar at the top of the Spreadsheet program. In Excel, Chart

Properties is under the Chart task bar item when you touch the chart. As a result, the Pareto Chart can be developed as below:

	Late Arr's	Accum	Rank
7 PM	10	10	1
6 PM	9	19	2
4 PM	9	28	2
5 PM	8	36	4
3 PM	7	43	5
9 AM	6	49	6
10 AM	6	55	6
2 PM	6	61	6
8 PM	5	66	9
1 PM	5	71	9
9 PM	4	75	11
12 AM	3	78	12
11 AM	3	81	12
8 AM	3	84	12

Run Charts

A graph that tracks performance over time or other measurement is a **Run Chart**. Effective run charts are used to visually compare rates of change or performance to a benchmark. The run chart graph following this paragraph represents the original data of the Pareto Chart, before the ranking and sorting process was developed.

You will see there are four lines graphed, the number of Late Arrivals, the "UCL" or Upper Control Limit, the "LCL" or Lower Control Limit, and the "Mean" or Average of all data graphed. The intent of the limits is to compare the data to benchmarks that are developed through a statistical measurement called "Standard Deviation."

However, before your eyes begin to gloss over, or your mind races to concerns that you are going to become a statistician, *Relax!* The reason we must talk about this subject is so that you can understand *how* measuring

definition

Run Chart:
A graph that tracks performance over time or some other measure used to visually compare rates of change or performance to a benchmark.

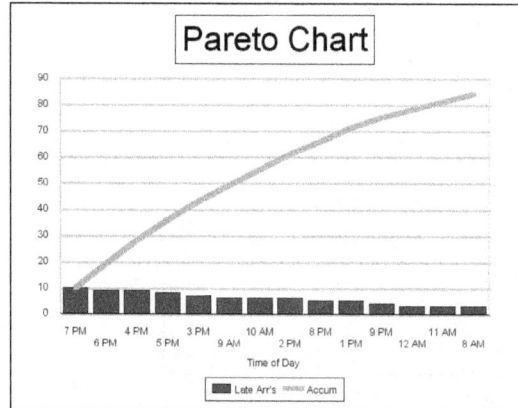

Pareto Chart

performance works! If you do not understand these words, try rereading them or ask questions during the class.

Standard Deviation (SD) is a statistical term for how much the data varies from the mean or average. That means how much of a change is a data point as compared to the mean. An example would be the average, or mean, of two numbers, 1 & 2, is 1.5. Since there are only two numbers, the SD is 0.5. If we were to add the number 3 to the list, the average would be 2, but the SD would be .8165, not 1, because the third number influenced the SD's formula. In Excel, it is found as "STDEV".

A meaningful Standard Deviation exists ONLY when the data values change from one measuring period to another. In other words, if you see that the temperature throughout the day does not change (it stays 50 degrees from morning to night), then a standard deviation is meaningless, because it is zero. However, if the temperature throughout the day changes frequently, then a standard deviation will measure *how much* of a change goes on during the day.

Why should we know the Standard Deviation (SD)? It helps a team to determine what to measure and what to compare those measurements to. For example, in our case of the Late Arrivals, the standard deviation for the data was 2.268. By itself, the SD means very little. However,

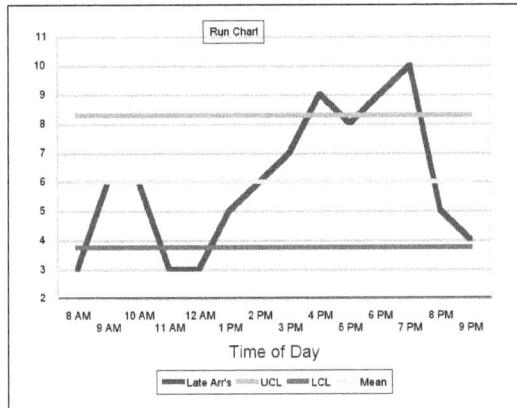

comparing the 2.268 with the "mean" or "average" and the data point in question makes the SD mean much more. Or let's talk about a hurricane off the shores of Florida that is creating BIG waves in Rhode Island. That difference in wave size indicates a problem that can't be seen nearby.

By *adding* the SD to the mean of 6, (2.268+6=8.268) you now have the Upper Control Limit (UCL) that allows you to view those events where the late arrivals broke above 1 standard deviation or 8.3 or more in that time.

The Lower Control Limit (LCL) is calculated by *subtracting* the SD from the Mean (6 - 2.268 = 3.732). The graph shows the Upper Limit, the Lower Limit, and the Mean or "Average." What this all translates to is that we should be paying very close attention to those times of the day when the late arrivals are either over 8.268, or less than 3.732. For the late arrival example, we should be studying very closely what happens at 8a, 11a, 12n, 4p, 6p, & 7p. By focusing on improving these times, we may develop systems to reduce the SD from 2.268 to a smaller number.

It is helpful to determine *why* these particular arrivals of the day exceed the limits. Over time, if we have problem-solved correctly, the Standard Deviation should shrink continuously (which is continuous improvement!), resulting in fewer variations and more consistent results. *Six Sigma* represents the shrinking of the Standard Deviation

TEAM TIP

The Standard Deviation helps a team to determine what to measure and what to compare those measurements to.

to a very small number. In other words, the performance is consistent and reliable, and the chance of having late arrivals exceed the average by much is very low.

Brainstorming Process
or How to Create Alternative Solutions

In the last few decades, much research involving the process of developing new ideas and creativity has emerged. Noted authors, Gary Hamel and CK Prahalad, wrote a book *Competing for the Future*, where they describe strategic planning processes with a focus on Competency, or "Set of Skills," Development. They viewed brainstorming as "Sense of Discovery," or the ability to discover new things or solve current problems better than the competition. Our intent with this book is to institutionalize these discovery processes into your day-to-day activities, so that your performance improves.

Brainstorming is an individual or group process whereby many ideas are generated without evaluation, in order to determine the best alternatives that will solve the problem. There are three primary approaches to improving the outcomes of a brainstorming session: "Round Robin," "Ballot Box," or the "Spontaneous " approach.

The **Round Robin** approach refers to the process of having each person on the team speak up without interruption, to share their ideas. It allows people to share their views, especially those who are less inclined to talk. However, without a skilled facilitator, those unwilling to share ideas will be left out.

The **Ballot Box** approach works much like a ballot voting process. Each person writes down his/her ideas on a piece of paper and submits them to the leader anonymously, who then collects the ballots and reads them to the members. This allows people to communicate those ideas that may not be politically correct or that might offend senior management.

The **Spontaneous Approach** refers to the concept that the idea creation is "free form" and there is fairly little structure to the process. The idea is to allow people to share ideas and build further ideas from those original ideas.

Doug Hall of Richard Saunders International is famous for developing new product ideas in less than 30 days. A remarkable feat since Proctor & Gamble takes over 90 days to develop new ideas. A writer for *Inc. Magazine* in May of 1997 portrayed Hall's brainstorming approach by following him around for 24 hours.

Here are some of the basic rules or concepts that help Mr. Hall and his team to help companies create new ideas:

1) No idea is bad.

2) Everyone is encouraged to participate.

3) Encourage free thinking by allowing people to stimulate their brains with humor, games, and "fun" activities. There should also be stimuli available to increase brain activity, such as pictures, magazines, and lots of blank paper.

4) In most cases, having flip charts or public presentations on the wall are far more effective for documenting the information and idea generation.

5) Many of the best ideas come as the end of the session nears, and new ideas have been all but exhausted.

6) Building on ideas generates new forms of ideas.

7) People must have the belief that anything is possible.

8) Good and bountiful food stimulates ideas.

9) Focus on quantity first, culling the weaker ideas and building on the remaining ideas later.

CONCLUSION

The challenge for increasing the pace of continuous improvement lies in the team's abilities to identify & brainstorm a problem's solutions more effectively. These methods we are teaching you are foundations for improved performance. As your teams evolve, they will need to acquire the Lean Six Sigma techniques of process and value stream mapping. The following are Lean principles for teams to follow: 1) Focus on the customer's benefit or value. 2) Identify and process map how the work gets done (the value stream); 3) Manage, improve and smooth the process flow; 4) Remove Non-Value-Added steps and waste; 5) Manage by fact and reduce variation; 6) Involve and equip the people in the process; and 7) Undertake improvement activity in a systematic way. In the next chapter, we will be covering how to build flowcharts or process maps, action plans or team charters and follow-up systems that will reduce the cycle time of corrective action.

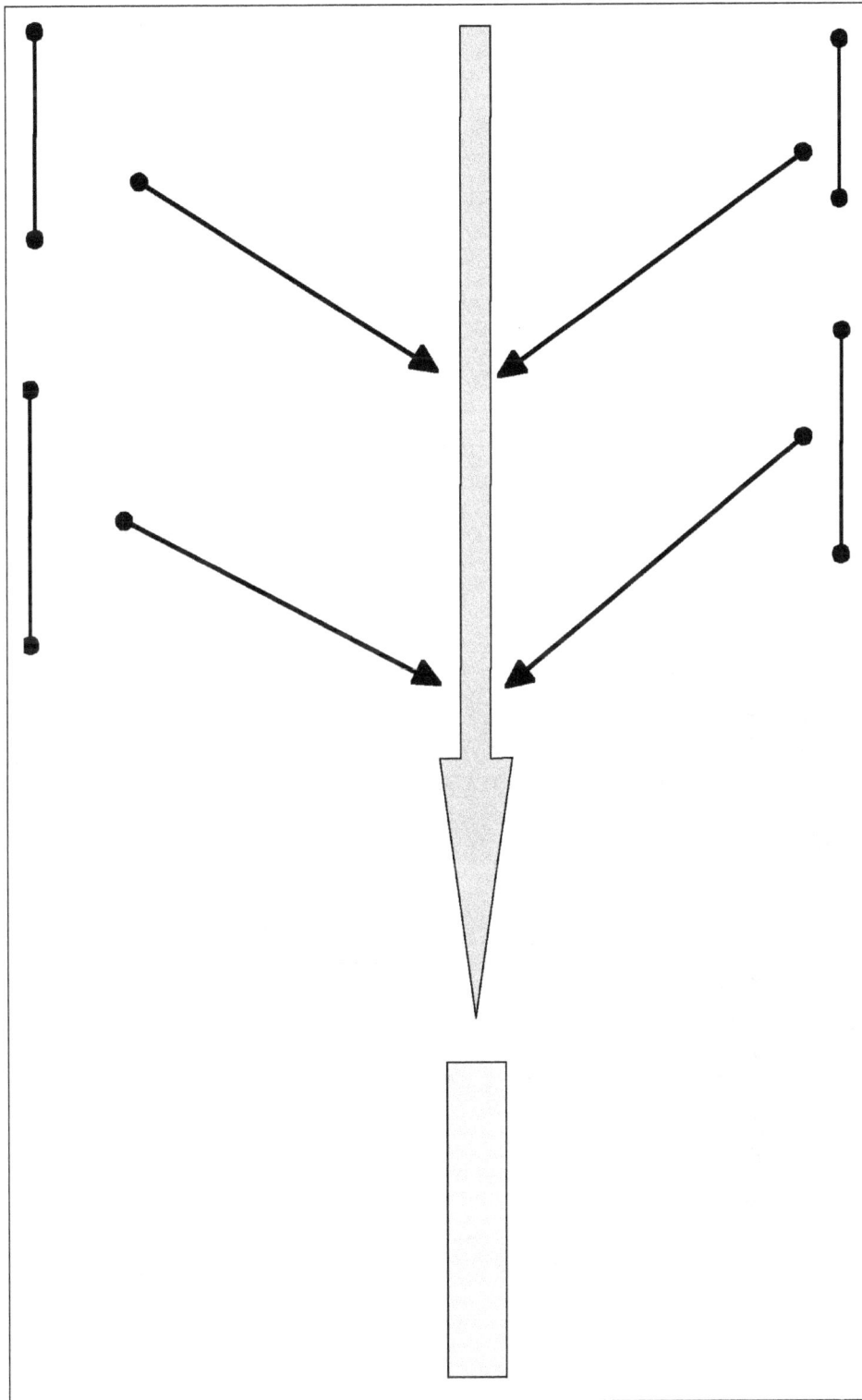

Homework Assignment #1

1) With the attached fishbone diagram, begin the process by taking one problem you know to exist in the company, and writing down the various causes and effects. For a review and example, please look at page 36.

2) With your Microsoft Excel spreadsheet, take the data on the attached back side of the fishbone and prepare a Pareto and Run Chart. Be sure to show the UCL & LCL, and the mean with the data. If you do not know how to use a PC spreadsheet, work with someone who does.

Homework Assignment #2

Prepare a graph using your spreadsheet program using the following data (the blank columns should be produced by you using Excel's "=Rank" & "=STDEV": Hint- the accum column is a formula that adds the accum data from the cell above the current cell plus the cell to the left.

Activity- # of Sales Orders by Hour	Data	Accum	Rank	UCL	LCL
7:00a	10				
8:00a	30				
9:00a	50				
10:00a	55				
11:00a	75				
12:00n	75				
1:00p	105				
2:00p	75				
3:00p	50				
4:00p	30				
5:00p	20				
6:00p	50				

CHAPTER 4

DEVELOPING PROBLEM SOLVING SKILLS
PART2: NORMING & PERFORMING

Learning Objective Questions from Chapter Three: Developing Problem Solving Skills. Part 1:Forming & Storming

✎	*What are the three basic categories of Problems?*
✎	*Describe the differences between them...*
✎	*What tools would you use to analyze possible causes of problems?*
✎	*What tools would you use to follow-up on the changes of implementation?*
✎	*On the fishbone diagram on page 37, what was the problem?*
✎	*What was the pinpointed area of concern?*
✎	*What is Pareto's rule?*
✎	*What is the difference between a Pareto Chart and a Run Chart?*
✎	*What are the suggested ways to brainstorm?*

DEVELOPING PROBLEM SOLVING SKILLS

PART 2: NORMING & PERFORMING

Introduction

In the last chapter, we covered the process that involves identifying the problem and brainstorming solutions. This chapter will cover the remaining part of the process: the "Norming" and "Performing" stages of teams. These are critical stages because they require commitment and execution of action plans and measurement systems.

Building Action Plans: Step 1- Identify Tasks

The most important process to improved performance is the development of the Action Plan. No matter what charts you use, or what brainstorming process is selected, the entire effort will fall flat on its face without an implementation plan or action plan. It is important to know what activities are required, step by step, and how these tasks relate to each other in a time line. There are several methods to performing action plans.

For a specific task to execute with multiple deadlines, a "GANTT" chart is most effective as it illustrates timelines by time periods, such as days or weeks. The most popular project management software, such as Microsoft's "Project Manager," uses the GANTT charting process.

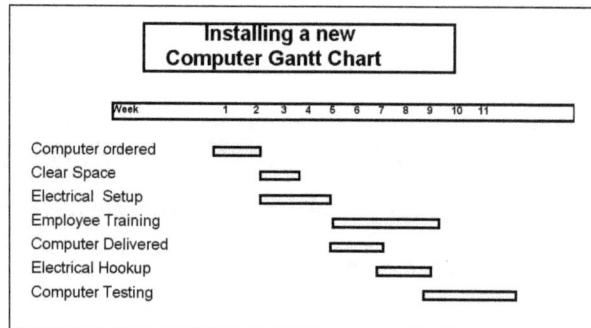

Installing a new Computer Gantt Chart

To set up a Gantt chart, the tasks must be identified, and then calculate the estimated time for each task taken. Further, each task must be placed at the given time period in which the efforts are to begin. Gantt charts (shown above) create a valuable graphic presentation of the project's timelines and tasks.

As you look at the Gantt chart above that relates to the Computer Installation, you will see that once the machine is ordered, clearing space and getting the electrical service begins. Once the computer is delivered, employee training begins, the electrical service is hooked up, and testing the computer begins. If the computer does not arrive on time, then the whole chart starting with employee training moves out. That, in turn, allows you to manage the electrician and training schedules in a more proactive way.

A "PERT" chart is more of a relational process illustration, where tasks are not related to time, but among each other. This is important for work process design, to identify those tasks that may not be as important or redundant.

Since a PERT chart illustrates processes as they relate to each other, The New Computer's process has three forks, each with their own stages. By using the PERT chart, you will find times where the same task is

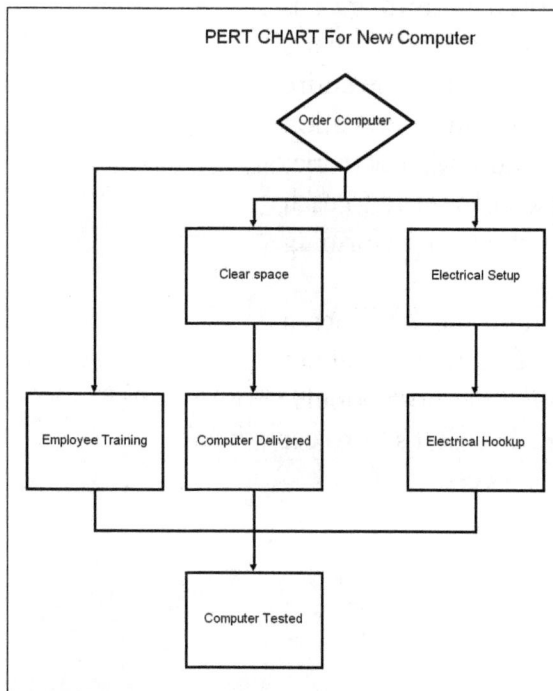

PERT CHART For New Computer

done over and over again, sometimes needlessly. The value of this charting process is to identify those tasks, procedures, and/or decisions that must be completed in the order in which they occur, and where they relate to the proceeding item.

By using a PERT chart in conjunction with a GANTT chart, it is possible to develop strategies for improving cycle times and reducing delays and redundant tasks. To succeed with continuous improvement, identifying and removing tasks is called "Changing Procedures," one of the three ways to reduce costs (the others being "Robotics" & "Training").

A **Procedure** is a series of steps or tasks that have a beginning and an end that usually involve a set of decisions. A **Process** is a group of procedures or related work activities that produce a value-added result. To illustrate the difference, let's use the example of a process called "Getting ready for work."

The above process map has several procedures and/or work activities, that can be mixed around in various orders. There is the "Wake up" procedure, the "Personal Hygiene" procedure, the "Getting Dressed" procedure, the "Nourishment" procedure, and the "Departure" procedure.

To save time, we will focus on one of these procedures, the "Wake Up" procedure. Please remember, procedures are defined steps or tasks with defined beginnings and ends. So, before we go any further, ask yourself the following, "What was the first thing you did to wake up this morning?" Stop here and write it down below:

_____
_____
_____
_____
_____
_____
_____
_____
_____
_____
_____

definition

Procedure:
A series of steps
or tasks that have
a beginning and an
end and that usually
involve a set of
decisions.

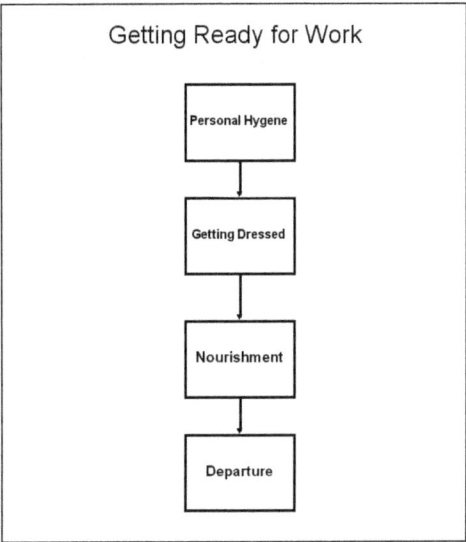

Getting Ready for Work

Personal Hygene

Getting Dressed

Nourishment

Departure

For some, it was setting the alarm "last night." For others, it was hearing the alarm and hitting the "snooze button." In our travels, we have discovered that people with a "darker side" of humor have other ideas for their wake up procedure, which we conveniently omitted. A properly developed set of procedures would be described this way:

1. Set the alarm before going to bed.

2. After the alarm goes off, and you hear it, respond as follows...

3. If you are facing the alarm with no obstruction (bed mate), take your free hand and place it over alarm's cover, grope for the buttons.

4. If you are not facing the alarm, roll over towards the alarm and follow step #3.

5. You need to decide whether or not you want to continue sleeping for 10 more minutes, or get up immediately.

6. Once you decide, execute the following:

7. If you want to wake up, shut off the alarm, or move the alarm to the "spouse alarm" slot.

8. Open your eyes, and with your free hand, pull the covers off yourself.

9. Move your feet to the floor; lift yourself off the bed; walk over to your bath robe; put it on, and go towards the bathroom.

10. If the bathroom is vacant, follow the Personal Hygiene Procedure.

11. If bathroom is NOT vacant, knock on the door, growl at the occupant, and advise him/her in kind words that you are waiting outside. Ask how much more time he/she plans on occupying the bathroom.

12. If not long, wait.

13. If a long time, go to Nourishment Procedure, or go to step 14.

14. If you choose to sleep in for 10 minutes, go back to sleep; repeat Step #2.

For those who have experienced the detail exercises of ISO 9000 implementation, you know how difficult defining procedures can be, let alone maintaining the descriptive tasks of each procedure. The illustration above represents the amount of detail needed to effectively define a procedure.

The reason for this detail is to provide an educational and training process for anyone else who may need to execute the same procedure. In other words, if you can do it, you should be able to teach the process to others. If you have mistakes or problems, it usually isn't the person, but the management system that is at fault (per Dr. Deming). Having clearly written procedures, along with decision trees (What if's), then you have the basis to improve the procedure or process. The challenge now becomes" "What to do next?"

Process Improvement involves the tactical implementation of change. It is not a strategic event, but a tactical one. Meaning that there is a mission, a focus, and defined objective. We have learned there are nine steps for successful and effective process improvement:

1. Define customer requirements.

2. Determine input requirements.

3. Define value-adding changes.

4. Flowchart current activity steps.

5. Analyze differences or variances, brainstorming for solutions.

6. Analyze cycle times to eliminate waste or redundancy.

7. Analyze compliance to project's mission.

8. Define, reconfigure, and implement new process.

9. Follow up and evaluate.

One of the most challenging areas of team building is changing the work process. We always hear "That's the way it is supposed to be done;" or "We have always done it that way," only to learn that people do not remember *why* they did it that way. Our approach is to look at every procedure and ask the following:

1. Do we need the procedure?

2. Does it copy somewhere else?

3. How much time does it take?

4. Is the result measurable?

5. Where will the Resistance to Change appear?

6. How can it be improved by using Process Change, Training or Robotics?

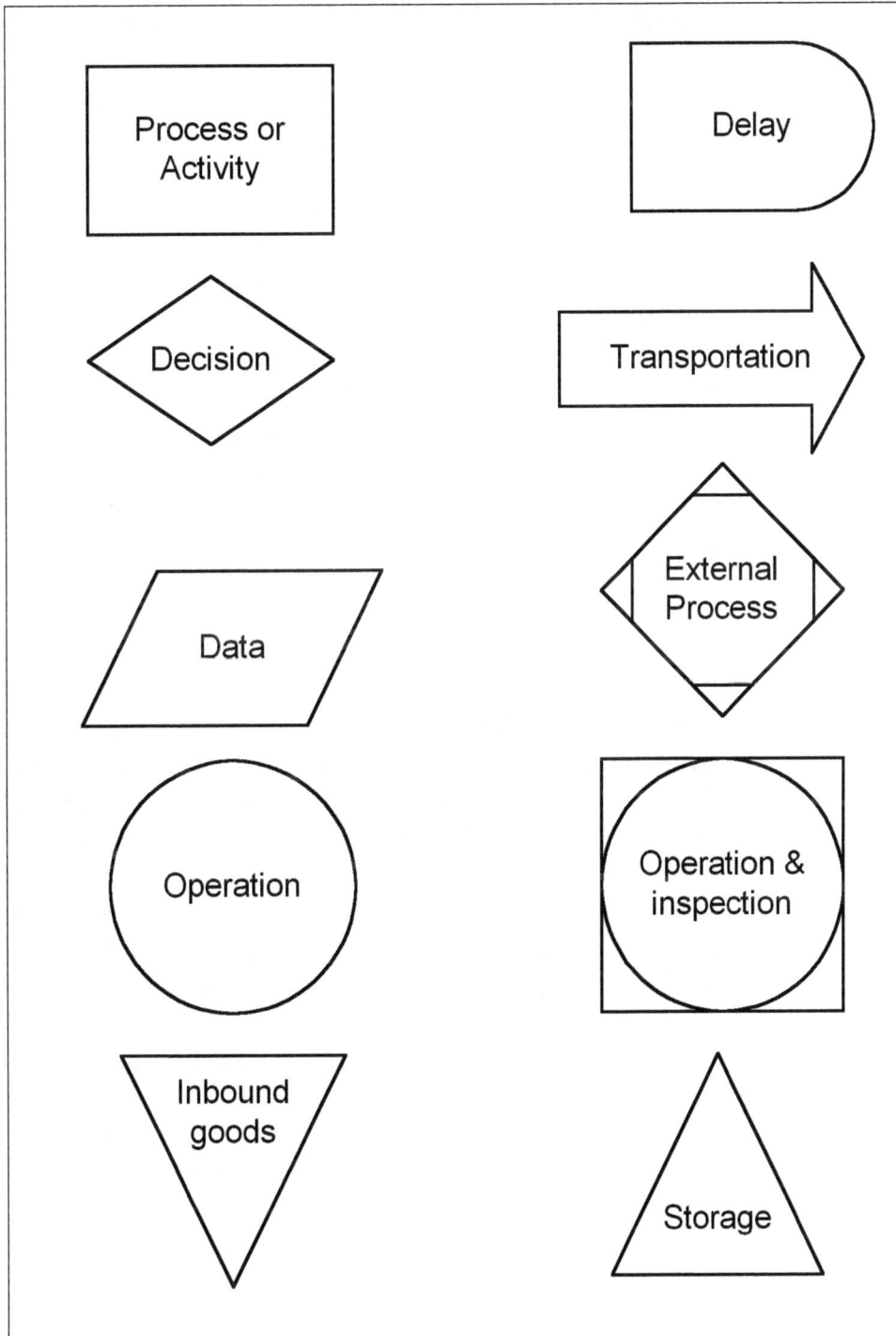

Building Action Plans: Step 2- Process Maps

Flow charting is a process whereby you graphically illustrate the decisions and activities using symbols. The PERT chart is a similar way to flow charting. However, flow charting is much more detailed about decisions, and other activities.

On the previous page, we have prepared a sample group of symbols that represent stages in a process. It is important that the flowchart represent *what currently works* rather than what it *could* or *should* represent. This distinction is important because we see debates develop over things like "if the activity in mind is actually occurring, or is it desired?" Team members will argue angrily over a procedure. We have consistently learned that what one person perceives is the activity is, in actuality, something else. Working in teams helps clarify issues.

Process Maps

A good way to demonstrate how a **Process Map** works is to illustrate the process of having people over for dinner. In the following example, you have asked your sister and brother-in-law over for dinner. After you asked them if they were available, you asked what food they were in the mood for, recognizing that your sister eats mostly vegetarian meals but her husband loves meat. As a result, the "girls and guys" tend to get along famously.

As you look over the diagram with the symbols on page 67, you will see where decisions, inspections, delays, and straight processes are illustrated. As you look closely at the graph, you will see that we did not go into much detail, such as how to prepare the salad because that would be a procedure.

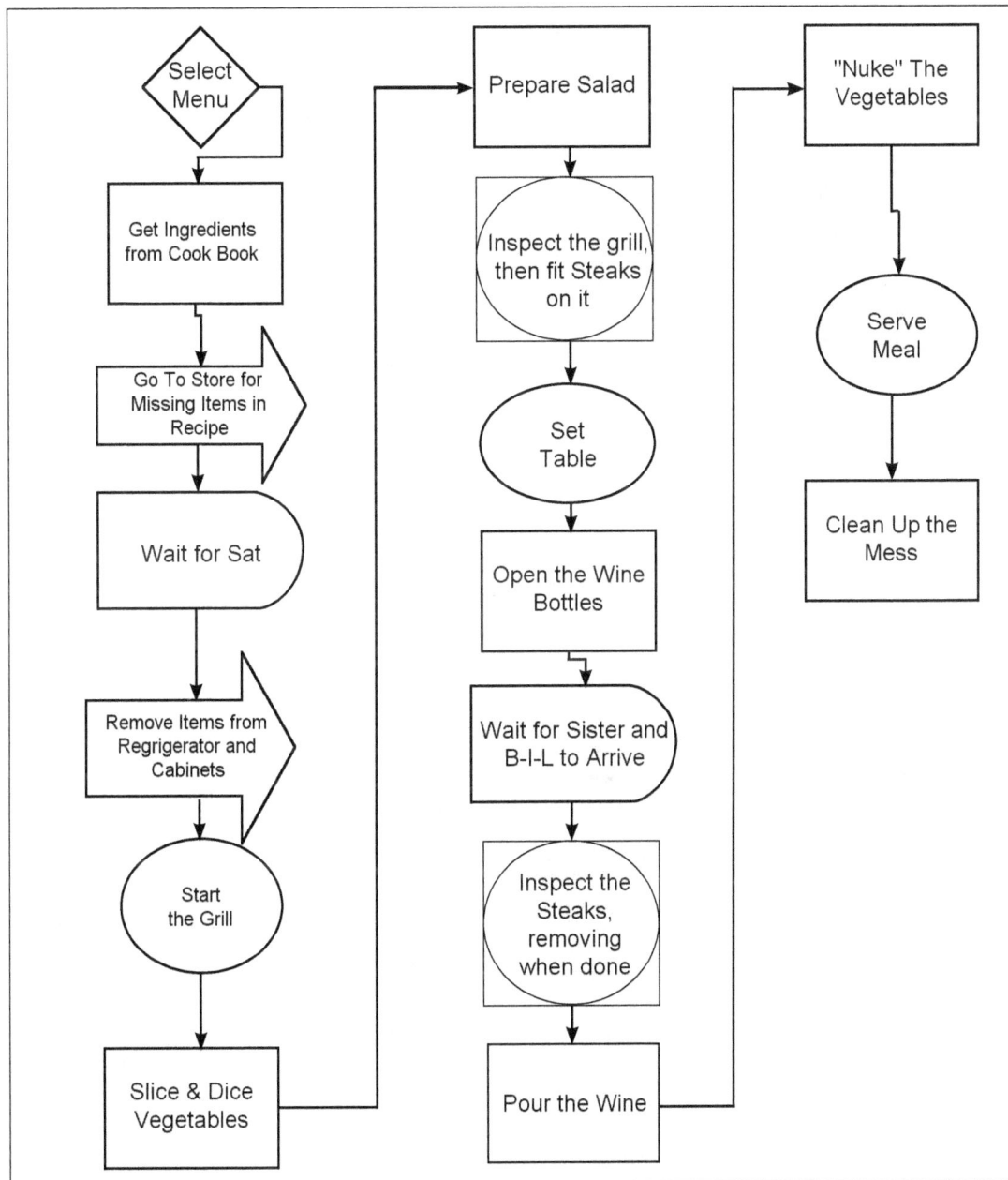

Relational Mapping

Relational Mapping refers to the development of a chart that shows a set of relationships and how flow passes through each relationship. In the case of the meal with your sister and

```
ME    [Select Menu]  →  [Get Ingredients from Cook Book]  →  [Go To Store for Missing Items in Recipe]

[Remove Items from Regrigerator and Cabinets]  →  [Prepare Salad]  →  ["Nuke" The Vegetables]  →  [Set The Table]

[Serve the Meal]  →  [Clean Up the Mess]

[Start the Grill]  →  [Slice & Dice Vegetables]  →  [Open the Wine Bottles]

My Spouse    [Pour the Wine]  →  (Inspect the grill, then fit Steaks on it)  →  (Inspect the Steaks, removing when done)  →  [Clean Up the Mess]

My Sister    [Wait for Sister and B-I-L to Arrive]  →  [Clean Up the Mess]
```

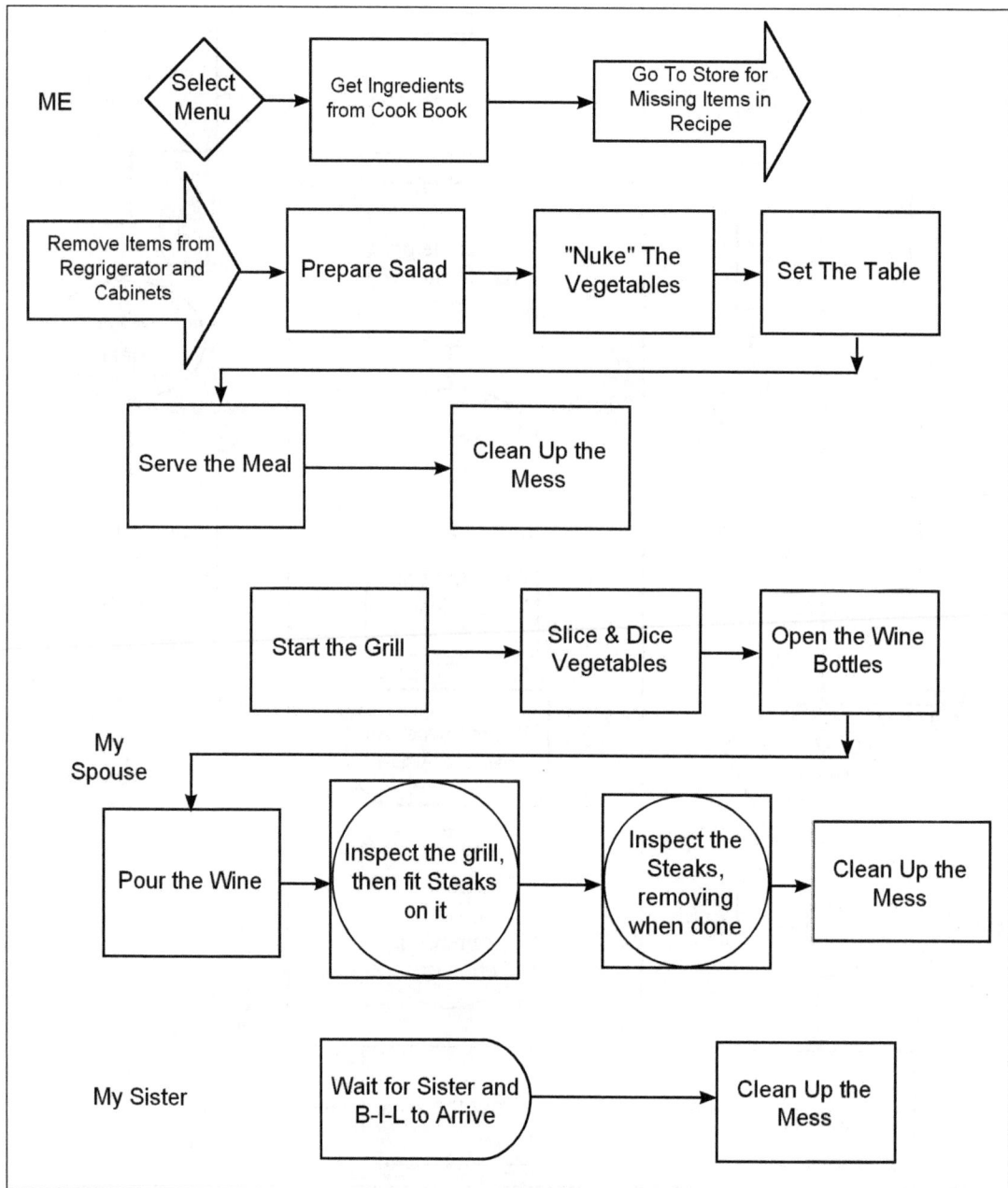

brother-in-law, the relational map would look something like the chart above.

The value of this type of illustration allows for who is involved with what, and the order in which they are involved. There are many types of relational map formats, but the context is to have each process relate to something or someone. Now that we have covered the basics of mapping, we will now focus on building the action plan.

Developing Action Plans

As a team, you have done all of your homework. You have: defined the problem, analyzed the data, mapped out the processes, and brainstormed new solutions. We discussed the process of problem solving by stages using tools, such as charting and pinpointing. Now is the time to implement a plan.

There are many books around that write about execution and implementation as a way to differentiate those people or organizations who succeed, from those who don't. We believe success comes from continually trying to improve things, by piloting small changes rather than large ones, and implementing those small changes well.

Building action plans effectively "Enables" High Performance Teams, as the plans provide goals and direction for team members, along with accountability and empowerment. There are several key elements for an effective Action Plan. They include:

1. **Heading of Worksheet:** describing the name of the team, who is the leader, and the date when the form was filled out.

2. **Problem Statement:** A Brief and Clearly written statement to describe the problem area to be addressed by the team.

3. **Clarify** if the result of the plan is to solve the problem, **recommend a solution,** or **develop research** for a problem.

4. **Task Description:** Now that you have developed a process map, begin identifying the specific tasks that will help solve the problem.

5. **Define the Team's Boundaries:** clarify the areas that do *not* involve the task of the team.

6. **Clarify** what the expected results or outputs should be.

7. **Outline** the resources required or needed to successfully execute this plan.

8. **Generate deadlines and key milestones** by date and/or task completion .

9. **Agree to the frequency of gathering together** or working on the project.

10. **List the Participants.**

11. **Confirm an evaluation:** Who will monitor the measurables, what will be monitored, and when will the evaluation begin and end.

TEAM TIP

In a team meeting setting, the team leader facilitates the discussion among the members to arrive at the answers for the plan's items.

In a team meeting setting, the team leader facilitates the discussion among the members to arrive at the answers for the plan's 11 items. Depending on the complexity of the problem or topic, building the action plan could take minutes or days.

If you find yourself in a meeting that has no meaning to you, you should be asking the leader at the end, in private, if there is someone else more valuable than yourself to replace you. However, if you are not contributing to the team, are not actively trying to solve the problem, and want to just do your job and go home, you may be a contributor to the problem and don't know it.

We have learned over the years that team development works when the participants want it to work. It requires sacrifice of time, ability to share, and the flexibility to change directions or try new things. The team system has worked in large and small companies because it enables good people to perform better. It also allows bad performers a chance to perform well with training and information sharing.

The next group of chapters relate to how the teams work. How do you get information from customers? How does the leadership lead a team? How do we measure ourselves properly? The first four chapters covered the tools, now we must explain how to use them.

Homework Assignment

There have been discussions in your management meetings over the years about getting a new phone system. The current system consists of a central telephone number going to a switchboard operator, who answers the phone and distributes it to an extension.

If no one answers, it rings back to the receptionist, who then takes the caller's name down and places the message in the person's "In-Box" of messages. Several new employees want voice mail, and direct extensions. This new system could cost over $10,000.

Since you use the phone, they have asked you to be on the "Phone Acquisition" team. Please use the symbols on page 69 and the chart on page 71 to describe how the old phone system works.

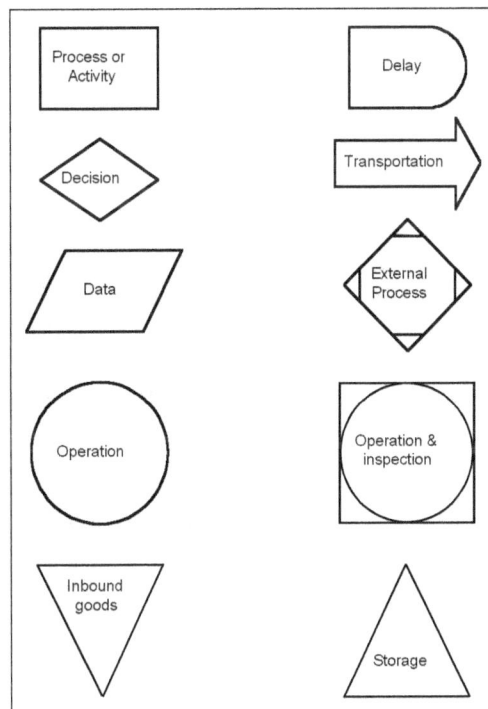

Process or Activity	Delay
Decision	Transportation
Data	External Process
Operation	Operation & inspection
Inbound goods	Storage

Action Planning Worksheet

Name of Team: _____ Date Formed: _____

Team Leader: _____

1) What is the problem to solve?

_____

_____

_____

_____

2) What is the team's mission? Solve ☐   Recommend ☐   Research ☐

3) What are the tasks involved?

A- _____

B- _____

C- _____

D- _____

E- _____

F- _____

4) What are the boundaries of this team's tasks?

_____

_____

_____

_____

5) What are the expected results or outcomes from this team's assignment?

_____

_____

_____

_____

6) How frequent will you meet? Daily ☐ Weekly (M ☐ T ☐ W ☐ Th ☐ F ☐ S ☐)

Other: _____ Time of Day: _____ Am ☐ Pm ☐ Duration: _____

Action Planning Worksheet (con.)

Name of Team

7) Deadlines: Start Date: End Date:

8) Key Milestones:

Date:	Milestone:
Date:	Milestone
Date:	Milestone:
Date:	Milestone:
Date:	Milestone:
Date:	Milestone:
Date:	Milestone:

9) Team Members (Don't forget to identify the Experts with an "X")

10) Follow-up: Sponsor Involved:

Initials and date of each Follow-up

What did Our company Learn from this Project?

CHAPTER 5

CUSTOMER REQUIREMENTS

Learning Objective Questions from Chapter Four: Developing Problem Solving Skills. Part 2:Norming & Performing

✐ | What is the difference between a process and a procedure?

✐ | What is a Gantt chart?

✐ | What is a PERT chart?

✐ | List below the 10 process map elements and their shape:

CUSTOMER REQUIREMENTS

Introduction

High performance management teams have **Customer Focus**. These teams know why their work is important and how their work fits in the total project. As mentioned earlier, Deming said "Quality" means 'Pride in Workmanship.' Quality is a term defined by customer expectations and requirements, rather than by a team's perceived ideas of what the customer wants. A team's focus on understanding customers and their needs and requirement will result in the positive feedback that "Pride" is based on. Innovation requires customer knowledge and understanding their needs.

In previous chapters, we mentioned that Drucker said, "The Purpose of a Business is to Create Customers!" He also said that there are two ways to create them: **Marketing** and **Innovation**. Innovation is about creating *new* or *better* ideas/products/services. Marketing refers to the activities relating to how a company communicates to, learns about, and develops relationships with customers to invite them to buy from you.

Our effort in this chapter is to focus on ways to improve a team's gathering of customer information. Be mindful that customers may include internal teams as well as outside vendors, suppliers, governmental agencies, and just about anyone who desires to use your product or service. Defining customers can be very confusing.

Step One:
Identifying Customers

Many times it is bewildering to determine the customer in the middle of a series of processes. A supplier or "partner" provides inputs to the team, and the team outputs to the customer. The most common approach to identifying customers is to go *outside* the team or company and find out who the paying customer or supplier is. For internal customers, the challenge is to make sure the output or services you create is going to a known final user; where the value of the output is at its highest, or the interaction is the most frequent or lengthy. If there are many customers to choose from, try using the Pareto rule of identifying the top 20%, where 80% of the value is generated by 20% of a list.

With the internet, the process of identifying customer segments, collecting information on buying habits or patterns, and testing new pricing models and promotions has greatly improved. With the use of "cookies," or small files that reside on a person's computer, a person's activities can be tracked. With a "brick and mortar" or stationary storefront concept, the store rarely knows more about the customer than the person's gender, possible age; and, if they are open to conversation, what they are looking for. In the case of a web-based storefront, a person can be tracked to see where they are going, if they have been to the site before, what products they bought before, and then is able to match similar, or complimentary products to the ones they have just purchased. The key is to identify the customer.

Once the customer is identified, the question of "Who owns the customer?" arises. It requires clear communication skills to articulate the reasons why one person or team owns the customer over another. Many times, several teams will own the customer, but the point of activity in which change will occur requires that the team closest to the process owns it.

The next step is to identify the customer's contact person, to whom your correspondence or communication is directed. This person is usually an assigned or frequently contacted person.

Asking Questions

You have identified your customer and their contact person. Now you must ask them questions to get **Feedback**. Marketing people will tell you that what and how you ask questions will influence the responses. The team should develop a list of questions that will provide insight to what the customer needs, wants, or expects. Some topics could include:

MARKETING

- ✔ What is the your team NOT doing now that the customer would like you to do?

- ✔ What is the your team doing now that the customer would like you to STOP?

- ✔ What is the your team doing now that the customer likes and wants to have continued?

- ✔ What changes are the customers making that you should be aware of and that may impact your team?

- ✔ In what areas are your team not meeting expectations or leaving your customer unsatisfied?

- ✔ How does your company compare to the competition with performance issues below?

With regard to performance issues, topics may include the following:

- ❑ **Accuracy**

- ❑ **Adaptability / Flexibility**

❑ **Availability**

❑ **Courtesy**

❑ **Pace of Action (Speed)**

❑ **Quality**

❑ **Quantity**

❑ **Responsive**

❑ **Timeliness**

Here are some suggested Interview Guidelines for effective responses:

☞ Clearly identify or explain to the customer which-team you are representing, and why you are interviewing them. You may have to educate the customer about your company's products or services.

☞ Use "open-ended" questions, such as "What do we do that you dislike?" to draw out answers that you may not have thought of. The focus is on performance and expectations.

☞ If you receive a negative response that bothers you, avoid any form of defensive reactions since the answers may be helpful, rather than harmful. DO NOT explain or defend, because the customer usually stops the interview as a result.

☞ Try to focus on the customer's response as "what the product/service should be," rather than "what is wrong."

☞If your customer responds in general terms, such as "Everything is okay, no problems," try to follow-up with more specific alternative questions to draw out further information. A question could be: "I appreciate that things are okay, any ideas about how we could improve quality or speed up responses?"

☞Ask your customer to allow your team to follow up with this survey with either an upgraded survey or feedback from the data generated after the survey is complete.

Feedback

There are four basic ways for teams to obtain feedback from the questions:

1. **Personal Interviews**: Asking questions directly of the customer with the chance to clarify information or responses is highly valuable. The drawback is that personal interviews take time and skill to draw meaningful information from a person. These interviews can be done face to face, over the phone, or using conferencing systems with internet or teleconferencing equipment. Include focus groups or teams using survey systems with video features found in Zoom, GoTo Meeting, Google Meet, and Microsoft Teams, just to name a few.

2. **Interactive Chat/Polling Apps:** In today's world of communications apps, such as SurveyMonkey, Turning Technologies, Zoho Survey, What's App, Google Hangouts, and Microsoft Teams, the ability to interview people through this technology can be as equally helpful as a personal interview, and structured as a written survey. The drawback to such an activity is the elimination of seeing the person's reaction or tone of voice. Further, the process of replacing the voice with typed words can

be slower and less accurate if the typist is not an accurate speller.

3. **Written Questionnaires:** Written questionnaires, either using multiple choice or open ended essay style answers may not be as interactive or insightful as a personal interview. However, they can be "anonymous" so that difficult answers can be made without fear of retribution. In some cases, the lack of response to questions or the inappropriate response to the question due to misunderstanding the question can be drawbacks to written surveys and questionnaires.

4. **Website / Electronic "E" Surveys:** There are several interactive and static survey processes for gathering survey data to choose from, such as customer reviews from a followup email outreach. Another is a Standard online "Click Here" answer process, whereby the participant picks a preset answer by touching a button next to the answer or has a "drop-down" list to choose from. The webserver then retains the information and sends it to the survey team automatically. By using a search engine you can find many sources of survey systems, such as surveymonkey or polldata. There is also a far more interactive approach using a combination of Java Scripting and E-commerce processing similar to "Grocery Cart" shopping on a retail site. The concept is to have the answers sent back to the webserver to be processed and a response to be sent back to the participant simultaneously. With a properly designed website survey, using buttons or Java scripts, the answers are formatted in a spread sheet layout, such as Microsoft's Excel or Lotus' 1-2-3 programs.

5. **"Cookies:"** As mentioned earlier, these are small files that collect data on a computer user or person.

They reside on the user's computer, usually in the folder area of the browser. Google uses cookies to track users or visitors as they journey throughout the internet. Google Analyitics is a free feature to display visitor profiles and activity. They also manage advertising campaigns and Google Adwords statistics. These cookies track things like how many times you, the user, have frequented the site, and where you have traveled throughout the site; it may keep your credit card info, so they know about your credit history or personal information, and cookies track your buying habits, such as commonly purchased book themes (i.e., fiction, business, or self-help).

It is important that simplicity and brevity be the foundation of a good survey. Most people cringe when they know the survey will take more than three to five minutes. In some cases, it is important to *reward* the interviewce with some gift or prize. The team wants meaningful information (Customer expectations and requirements) and the participant wants to go on to other things quickly.

Analyzing the Data

The survey questions have all been returned and set up on templates, spread sheets, or databasing formats. The data is then separated into *four* categories:

A. Feedback relating to ongoing activities or measurement systems that do not require "Storming, Norming, and Performing."

B. Feedback belonging to other teams.

C. Feedback that will allow for a "Quick Fix" exercise, whereby the team's response is to fix or resolve an easy issue, early, and quickly.

D. Feedback that involves issues that involve the four full stages of problem solving as described in previous chapters.

The team should be working together reviewing the data, discussing how to categorize each type, and the relevance of answers that may be in question. Meetings at this stage can be lengthy, depending on how the data are formatted and presented. Debates may last for days as the feedback is discussed and brainstorming efforts evolve. The chart below is an example of a customer loyalty survey covering 200 companies. Is your firm building satisfaction to increase sales or repeat business?

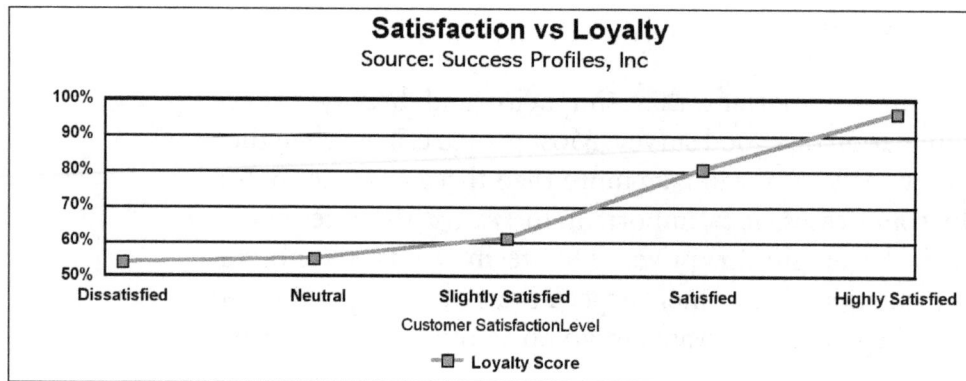

Satisfaction vs Loyalty
Source: Success Profiles, Inc

	Dissatisfied	Neutral	Slightly Satisfied	Satisfied	Highly Satisfied
Loyalty Score	54%	55%	60%	80%	95%

Customer Satisfaction Level

In conclusion, focusing your interviews or data collection methods on "What things should be" rather than "What's wrong" will help your team's brainstorming sessions move quickly and productively. The data, properly formatted, can develop into the basis of "norming" or measuring systems. Don't forget the old saying in relationship marketing: "People buy from People. Focus on a customer's **needs** for change and sales/profitability growth." The ultimate sale is one where you sell value, not products or services. Understanding the clients needs comes first.

EXERCISE

Chapter 5: Customer Requirements

In preparation for the next chapter, please answer the following questions based on YOUR Point of View:

Please list your Department's internal and external customers by class or group.

Please explain what your team's products and services are to each customer group, and how you communicate to them.

What do you believe to be the most important expectations or requirements those customers are desiring your team to fill?

How should your team anticipate future needs that your customer may desire?

CHAPTER 6

MEASUREMENTS & SCORECARDS

Learning Objective Questions from Chapter Five: Customer Requirements

In your company, who are the customers by each functional area?

What are the the basic ways to improve interview effectiveness?

What kind of ways can you get feedback?

Describe your company's way of measuring customer satisfaction or loyalty?

MEASUREMENTS & SCORECARDS

Introduction

As you watch a sports event—basketball for example—you will find the coach and players watching the scoreboard during the game. There are several measurements posted that capture their interest. The primary measurement is the score of the game. There is also the time left in the period, as well as which period the game is in. In some cases, there are individual player statistics, such as the number of fouls, points, rebounds, and free-throws. The meaning of the game is to *Win*. The final score is the measurement, but one game does *not* make a season.

This chapter is about building the correct measurements that relate to how your company *Wins*. The scorecards you build should reflect individual and company performance. It should be noted that games come and go, but the season must have more *Wins* than *Losses*. It is about creating a purpose and direction that everyone can focus on, and then create results towards that direction.

When comparing an individual's measurements to a team's results, conflicts usually arise. In Eli Goldratt's book, *The Goal*, a boy scout team that was walking through the woods represented a measurement system. If the fastest kids made it through the woods, while the slowest person did not, then the team wasn't working to *Win*. The individuals were working for themselves. To *Win*, the entire Team had to make it to the destination *together*.

In a related story, the Boston Celtics' owner and coach, Red Auerbach selected players who individually worked well as a team, rather than on how well they performed individually. Winning required the ability to play defense, as well as offense. Players had to know how to pass the ball, rebound, and create steals, along with being able to shoot. He focused on team statistics rather than individual numbers. In another study, it was found that college teams without names on the game jerseys had far more winning seasons than did those schools with names on game jerseys.

Decades ago, the late Tom Landry and the Dallas Cowboys developed a computer-driven data collection process that provided numerous statistics on their own team plays, and their players' statistics, along with information about their competitors. They also developed forecasting models to predict competitor's plays and to identify trends in play making and individual performance. Other NFL coaches and teams thought this type of effort was a waste of time, resulting in numerous jokes about the computer. After several years of success in Dallas, the jokes faded. Today, *every* NFL team has computer models and works them religiously. However, we do *not* endorse coaches or teams to videotape opponents call signals as a method of improving performance.

This chapter is about the process of developing the most meaningful information, so that teams can track performance. Creating measurements and scorecards help motivate teams with a purpose and direction, to create "winning" results, and to develop problem-solving skills for improved performance.

Information or Data

We have found that confusion sets in when people use the terms **Data** and **Information**. These words are not interchangeable. *Data* refers to the collection of random measurements that can be grouped, ranked, sorted, or related to other data in a way to create information. *Information* is the interpretation or analysis of the data that decisions are based on after they have been sorted, grouped, or ranked. Information is organized data, or "Feedback."

An example is an Invoice number 12345 for $100. That is Data. Knowing it is either a purchase invoice or sales invoice may also be data. Knowing that it is grouped

---

definition

Data:
collection of random measurements that can be grouped, ranked, sorted, or related to other data in some way.

Information:
organized data or 'feedback'.

INVOICE

Date: 01/01/2000

Invoice #: 12345

$100 For Services and Products Rendered

---

by a product or service number, by month, by customer, or region allows this invoice to now become information.

When developing scorecards, the measurements must be translated into information. Effective scorecards should have the following characteristics to be successful:

✓ Scorecards must have clearly defined and measurable performances or results as part of the design. In other words, a score that can be challenged for accuracy or meaning to a customer is an ineffective score. *Example: Waste output is not as clear as scrap rate with units per hour, or per work order.*

✓ Performances or Results must have importance or significance to motivate change when the information indicates unsatisfactory results. *Example: Cycle time per work order may not make sense to a machinist or shipper. It may be very important to an expediter.*

✓ The measurement system must be consistent and frequent in order to solve problems quickly and with reliable feedback. *Example: Measuring rejected parts once a month may not stop a growing vendor trend in time.*

✓ Effective scorecards are displayed visually, and usually track desirable results or behavior in a positive, rather than negative way. Many times, graphs and charts are placed in prominent locations for all to read and see. *Example: Run charts on attendance are more preferable than absenteeism, deliveries on time rather than late deliveries, profitability rather than losses.*

What to Measure?

Here is a sample list of measurements:

Customers/Sales:
- Number of New Customers
- Number of Lost Customers
- Customer Satisfaction Survey Results
- Customer Complaints by Category
- Repeat Business
- Avg Dollar per Order
- Number of Quotes/ Orders
- Market Share
- New Products Introduced
- Sales Volume Comparatives
- Budget Comparisons
- Order Entry Errors
- Change to Orders
- Quote to Order Cycle Time
- Takt Time (Customer Demand Rate)

Production/Operations:
- Output per Time Unit
- Cost per Unit
- Vendor Rejection Rate
- Quality/Accuracy
- Equipment/Machine Utilization
- Budget Comparisons
- Overtime
- Takt Time (Customer Demand Rate)
- Slack Time (Time between Activities)
- Shipping/Delivery Rates
- Inventory Shortages/Substitutions
- Rework or Damage Rates
- Cross Training Rates
- Work Order Changes

It is important that the teams identify a group or family of measurements, rather than one single master measurement. These groups of measurements should be aligned with the goals and objectives of the company and the teams. Depending on the objective, the measurements should have an impact on the customer's view of value. Be reminded that a principle behind scorecards is to improve performance and motivation through shared information and common purpose or focus.

Clerical or professional scorecards have different performance measurements and customer expectations than a manufacturing or distribution company. These scorecards are usually broken down into the following groupings:

Projects: Long Term. Projects requiring significant planning and scheduling activities, such as Product Development, Product, or Market Research, Mergers/ Acquisitions, and Core Competency Development.

Projects: Repeating. Activities that continually show up to be done, such as monthly or annual reports, website updates, payroll, or billing.

Projects: Short (Fast) Term. Activities that involve quick turnarounds, and less planning and scheduling, such as marketing campaigns, special reports, and expediting problems.

Operations. These activities involve the production of work, such as data entry, file updating and document filing, and technical or customer support.

Support Functions. These activities relate to the non-operational efforts, such as office maintenance, training, and planning or scheduling.

Collecting Data, Building Scorecards

You have just finished eating at a restaurant; and, along with the receipt, the server gives you a customer survey card. If you throw it away, does the management team learn anything from you? Do you care? You are a customer;

> **definition**
>
> *Operations:* activities that involve the production of work, such as data entry, file updating and document filing, and technical or customer support.

how should the server and the manager encourage you to cooperate? Why should they bother? Were the questions the ones that you wanted to answer?

The challenge of any organization is to make sure 'what they measure and how they measure it' makes sense. Any of the measurements on the previous page are useless, unless the customer sees value in wanting it that way. How many times have you returned to a restaurant because the people were important to you, not the quality of the food. What about the atmosphere, the quantity of food, the nearby location, or if your kids want a restaurant for the toys or a special promotion? Measuring performance for any of these questions requires more than a simple survey or cash register receipt.

The key is collecting data from customers. In the last chapter, we learned that **Feedback** relates to the information you get from a customer, in order to improve processes or the quality of a product or service. Once the customer explains what is important to them, it is important to begin evaluating the company's processes to insure alignment in performance, value, and expectations. If the customer does not care about speed of service, should you measure it? If the customer wants quality rather than quantity, should you measure the food as it arrives by quantity or quality?

It is very important to separate scorecards or measurements by either activity or behavior. In a restaurant, behavioral measurements are qualitative in nature, while activity measurements relate to cycle times and queue times for sitting, ordering, cooking, serving, and closing of the meal. Try to remember this motto: *"It's WHAT you measure and HOW you measure it that counts!"* We have learned that when people get lost in the numbers and measurements, the final outcomes are wrong.

Balanced Scorecards (BSC)

The Balanced Scorecard concept was developed by David Norton and Richard Kaplan in their book *The Balanced Scorecard.* They developed this process in order to align the key business issues and goals. They learned that successful companies used more than one measurement to gauge their performance in consistent and similar ways. To many, this form of measuring value is very hard to understand. Our attempt is to help you with this concept.

BALANCED SCORECARD WORKSHEET			
Performance Indicator (KPI)	**Measurement**	**Data Source**	**Goal/Comparison**
Operational Measurements:			
Volume	Units/hour	Production Rprt	200 units/Hr
Costs	$/Units	Cost Report	15% reduction
Customer Satisfaction Measurements:			
Turnaround Time	Days Wait	Quote Log	24 Hr Turn
Faster Delivery	Workorder Days	Workorder Rprt	14 days
Shareholder measurements?			
Financial Return	Return on Equity	Bal. Sheet/P&L	S&P500- 18%
Growth	Sales	Sales Reports	15%
Innovation measurements?			
New Products	# of New Prods	Sales Reports	5
Learning	% Cross Trained	Emp Reviews	50%

A Balanced Scorecard is a scorecard that provides simultaneous measurements for **shareholder values, customer satisfaction, operational goals,** and **learning/ innovation goals**. The key element is to have all indices reflect the goals of the company *together*. In this page's illustration of a BSC worksheet where a team is working on all of the measurements shown, the needs of the customer should be served as well as the company's.

The **Shareholder's** perspective involves measurements and goals that reflect financial returns and stock values. They are usually stated in terms of rates of return on equity, assets, or yields on investments or projects.

The **Customer's** perspective measures customer growth or performance, such as market share, number of complaints or returns, and amount of repeat business.

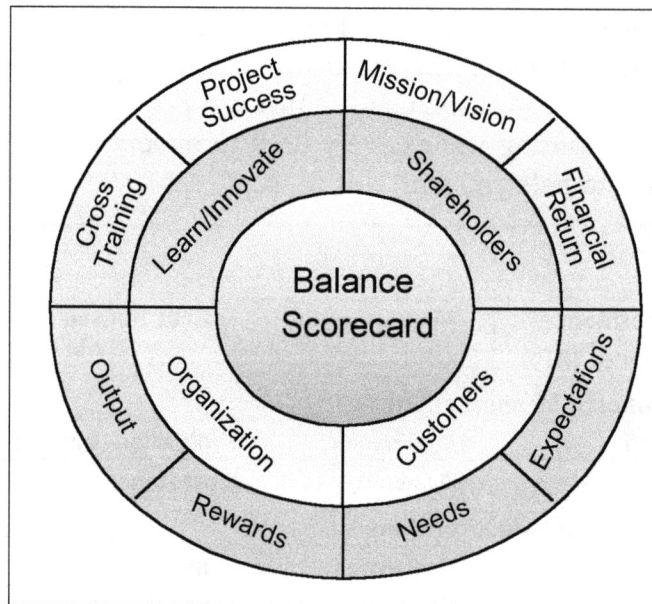

Be mindful that customers are not always the end users, but could be other internal departments or work stations. It is critical that the measurements have a connection to the end user too.

The **Operational** measurements relate to throughput and process goals, such as cycle times, costs per unit, or order fulfillment time.

The **Learning/Innovation** goals represent the company's ability to improve problem-solving abilities and to create new ideas for change. Examples include the number of new ideas implemented, number of employees cross-trained, number of new projects finished, and number of jobs filled from within the company.

The BSC is designed to illustrate and measure the health and performance of the business. It helps connect the cause and effect issues with high level goals. One purpose of using the BSC is to develop Key Performance Indicators or KPI's. KPI's are then posted for all to see and measure themselves by.

Whether you are measuring costs of scrap or profitability by product, the key to developing scorecards is to make sure the numbers you select for performance align with the company's overall goals. Our experience with Balance Scorecards has been not all satisfactory. We have discovered in many cases that the balance scorecard is flawed, because it does not connect individuals with corporate goals. We have witnessed some organizations using this BSC format resulting in reductions in sales or revenue, and fear then consumes the organization. We added this concept so you could know that it exists, since it does help some organizations to implement change much faster. The key is to have TEAMS develop and implement, rather than management.

Profit & Loss

During the time of Columbus, a monk developed a bookkeeping process of double entry that today is the basis of modern accounting. The words "debit" and "credit" are the common language of bookkeeping, often used with confusing and/or improper usage. The rule in double entry accounting is: if you have to make a debit, you must make a credit by the same amount, and vice versa. For example, if you deposit $100 into a checking account for invoice 12345, you will debit $100 to checking, and credit invoice/sales for $100.

A **Debit** represents an asset or expense increase. A **Credit** represents a Liability, Equity, or Income Increase. In all cases, a company wants to have more credits than debits in the equity and income area than debits. Why? Let's review how debits and credits work in a financial statement.

A typical **Financial Statement** involves two worksheets: a **Balance Sheet** and **Income Statement**. A balance sheet has three separate groupings: **Assets, Liabilities,** and **Owners Equity**.

Assets are those items that bring value to the business. On a personal point of view, the value of your house is an asset. Other assets include the cash value of a life insurance policy, money owed by a customer, and cash in the bank, as well as any property and equipment.

A **Liability** is an item that the company owes to a third party. Liabilities are usually debts or payables that the company has an asset to cover for it. Examples of liabilities

Owner's Equity: the difference between the assets, those items that bring value to the business, and liabilities, an item that the company owes to a third party, usually debts or payables covered by an asset.

include: the mortgage on a house, a vendor invoice not paid and owed, or taxes due, but not paid.

Owners' Equity or (OE) is the difference between the assets and liabilities. If the house is worth $200,000, and the owners owe $150,000 to a mortgage lender, then the owner's equity is worth $50,000. With the example above, owner's equity is the difference in total assets of $650,000 less the liabilities of $400,000 for a total OE of $250,000.

Compare Property, Plant, and Equipment of $600,000 with Mortgages of $350,000, and you will see that the $250,000 is *more* than owner's equity. **Depreciation,** or the reduction of value of an asset, is what drives the owner's equity down, as the assets *Decrease* in value. Depreciation is the formula that allows a company to expense off assets as they are used, since they will need to be replaced at some point in the future. It should be noted that depreciation is a tax deductible item that does not eat up cash, as compared to utilities or repairs. It is an amount developed by your CPA or audit firm that follows **Generally Accepted Accounting Practices**, otherwise known as GAAP.

Sample Balance Sheet for XYZ Corporation					
Assets			**Liabilities**		
Cash	1,000		Accounts Payable		30,000
Accounts Receivable	57,000		Accrued Taxes		2,000
Inventory	25,000		Bank Line of Credit		15,000
Prepaid Expenses	2,000		Misc Accruals		3,000
Total Current Assets	**85,000**		**Total Current Liabilities**		**50,000**
Property Plant & Equipment	600,000		Mortgage Payable		350,000
Vehicles	100,000		**Total Liabilities**		**400,000**
Office Equipment	50,000				
Less Depreciation	-250,000		**Owner's Equity**		
Total Fixed Assets	**500,000**		Stock		11,000
			Retained Earnings		189,000
Goodwill	15,000		Current Year Net Profit*		50,000
Amortization	50,000		**Total Owner's Equity**		**250,000**
Total Assets	**650,000**		**Total Liabilities & OE**		**650,000**
*Note- Net Profit on Balance Sheet equals Net Profit on Income Statement Page 103					

An Income Statement has five basic groupings: *Income or Revenue*, *Cost of Good Sold (COGS)*, *Operating Expenses*, *Financial Items*, and *Taxes*. From these groupings, subtotals, or totals are developed. Subtract COGS from Income and it will be called **Gross Profit**. Subtract Operating Expenses from

Income Statement for XYZ Corporation		
Sales		900,000
Less Discounts	-25,000	
Total Sales		**875,000**
Beg. Inventory	100,000	
Purchases	300,000	
Direct Labor	200,000	
Ending Inventory	-125,000	
Total COGS		**475,000**
Gross Profit		**400,000**
Sales & Marketing	90,000	
Office Expenses	18,000	
Office Payroll	100,000	
Vehicle Expenses	22,000	
Building Repairs	30,000	
Depreciation	25,000	
Utilities	35,000	
Total Expenses		**320,000**
Operating Profit		**80,000**
Debt Interest	10,000	
Interest Income	5,000	
Financial Items		**5,000**
Profit Before Tax		**75,000**
Taxes	25,000	
Net Profit*		**50,000**
*Net Profit above equals Net profit on Pg 102		

Gross Profit, and it will be called **Operating Profit**. Subtract Financial Items from Operating Profit, and it will be called **Profit Before Taxes**. Finally, when you subtract taxes from Profit Before Taxes, it is called **Net Income**, or **Profit after Taxes.**

Please Note that the Net Profit for XYZ Corporation is equal to the Current Year's Net Profit in the Balance Sheet shown on the previous page. There is a reason for this. Since all debits are usually assets and expenses, and all credits are usually liabilities, owner's equity and income, net profit is both a credit and owner's equity! If you add up all the debits of both the balance sheet and income statement and subtract all the credits from both, it will add up to ZERO! This is how proper business accounting works as a measurement system.

Some rules and usages to work by:

1. If ending inventory is adjusted down by $25,000 due to spoilage or shrink, then COGS will increase by $25,000 and Gross Profit *and* Net Profit will *drop* by $25,000. As a result, a rule of thumb is: *an inventory value reduction produces a reduction in profit*.

2. Working Capital (WC) is equal to the difference between current assets and current liabilities. (85,000 - 50,000 = 35,000) Therefore, it is important that WC is greater than -0- otherwise there is trouble ahead for paying vendors.

3. Cash flow is equal to net profit plus depreciation, or with XYZ Corp., cash flow is $75,000 (50,000+25,000). It is important that this number be positive as well. There will be times that a company will show NET LOSSES, but strong positive cash flows as depreciation is greater than the losses.

4. The Acronym EBITDA means "Earnings Before Interest, Taxes Depreciation, & Amortization" and is a very important number when a company needs to borrow money from a bank. It must be greater than the potential debt payment, otherwise the company will not be able to make the debt payments.

When a company goes to the bank and asks for a loan, the bank usually asks for "loan covenants" that include ratios relating to the financial statements. Listed below are a sample of formulas most bankers ask for.

Liquidity Ratios: Those ratios that measure the company's ability to generate cash.

> **Current Ratio:** *"Current Assets divided by Current Liabilities"* (85,000 / 50,000 = 1.7) Any number over 1 means that the company's ability to pay bills is good, but under 1 is usually a cause for concern.

> **Receivable Days:** *"Accounts Receivable Times 365 days divided by a full year of Sales."* (57,000 X 365 / 875,000 = 23.8 days) This number is compared to industry standards, with usual numbers being 10, 30, or 60.

> **Inventory Turns:** *"Cost of Goods Sold (Annual Material only) divided by Ending Inventory."* (300,000 / 25,000 = 12) This measurement expresses the number of times inventory is replaced or "turned." The higher the number, the more efficient the use of dollars.

definition

Inventory Turns:
This measurement expresses the number of times inventory is replaced or *turned*.

Operating Ratios: Ratios that help measure and evaluate management performance.

> **Return on Equity (ROE):** *"Net Profit or Income divided by Owner's Equity"* (50,000 / 250,000 = 20%). A high ratio or percent usually expresses effective management performance, while a lower number can indicate either a highly capitalized or conservative management. This ratio is usually compared to stock market returns.
>
> **Return on Assets (ROA):** *"Net Profit or Income divided by Total Assets"* (50,000 / 650,000 = 7.7%) A high ratio means that management is effectively managing assets or resources to produce income. This ratio is usually compared to industry data.
>
> **Debt to Equity (D/E):** *"Total Liabilities divided by Owner's Equity"* (400,000 / 250,000 = 1.6) A ratio of greater than 1.0 means that the company is "leveraged" or is relying on other people's money to increase profits. Ratios greater than 5.0 are considered very risky, and usually require higher ROI's to cover for the risk. Ratios of less than 1.0 indicate a company's strength to withstand hardship or economic downturns are good.

Every industry has its own measurements that best indicate management performance or company strength. Whether the company is a Manufacturer, Auto Dealer, Fuel Oil Dealer, Parts Distributor, Publishing Company, or Storefront Retailer, it is important that the management team identify the key performance indicators that will help measure improved performance.

Homework Assignment

Using the chart provided, write down several *Key* measures that you think best reflect your company or team's balanced view of your business.

Balance Scorecard

	Performance Indicator	Team Measurement	Data Source	Goal Comparison
1				
2				
3				
4				
5				
6				
7				
8				
9				
10				
11				
12				

Define your Customer Satisfaction Goals: _____

_____

_____

Define your Business Goals: _____

_____

_____

CHAPTER 7

IMPLEMENTING
CHANGE

Learning Objective Questions from
Chapter Six: Measurements & Scorecards

What is the difference between Information
and Data?

What are the four Elements of the Balance
Scorecard and the key measurements for each?

1)

2)

3)

4)

What are the THREE key areas or groupings of
the Balance Sheet?

What are the EIGHT key areas of the Income
Statement?

What is the Difference between a liquidity ratio
and an operational ratio?

IMPLEMENTING CHANGE

Introduction

This chapter is placed here, rather than at the end of the CSI workbook, because now is the time to begin working, rather than reading or talking. If you have followed the lessons to this point, you will have learned the basics to problem solving, process mapping, and building action plans. You will have basic knowledge in measurement systems and benchmarking formats. Your knowledge of the purpose of teams and organizing them will position you and your teammates to begin the process of change.

Usually at this point, we will have begun to build a strategic plan, or, at least, to form teams to prepare you for the work of the development process. The following chapters are more conceptual, and provided to help build the cultural values and to complete the vision that best describe your organization. In growing companies, the organization's ability to remain flexible, adaptable, and to indoctrinate the new staff members is what separates success from failure for the firm.

Change is driven by internal as well as external forces. The Second Law of Thermodynamics states that "the degree of disorder, or 'entropy' of an isolated physical system always increases." In other words, a physical system's degree of disorder or problems, such as a person or team, is directly related to the degree of isolation the physical system has, in relationship to the surrounding environment. For example, isolation cells in prisons create mental havoc for the prisoners. By the late 1980s and early '90s, IBM became so insular in their approach toward customers and technology that customers were leaving them in droves. It took a group of "Outsiders", including Lou Gerstner to create the change necessary to recreate a growth company again.

A living being or organization is considered "mature" when the body can no longer reproduce or regenerate quickly enough to replace dying cells or tissues. In a corporate body, maturity arrives when the organization's systems and processes stop adapting at the pace at which the market is changing. A comparison between two such companies is GOOGLE and Microsoft. Both grew fast and furious using software—but using different platforms—the internet and the PC.

By following the workshop provided by this CSI workbook, and by inviting outsiders into your company to help you, the chances are less likely that "disorder" or "maturity" will occur. Arrogance is described as the inability to hear or accept other points of view. Most successful companies lose sight of their vision, as they find success and then restrain the change that brought about success. This chapter both reviews this process and prepares you and your team to accept change and embrace it.

Theory "O" vs Theory "E"

Our experience tells us that most organizations believe that they must either change or die, as market threats force them to change. The pace of change has clearly risen with the evolution of the internet processes. There are two primary theories of change: **Theory E**: 'E' meaning *Economic Value*, and **Theory O**: 'O' meaning *Organizational Capability*.

Theory E changes are based on economic issues, such as shareholder value. It is usually known as the "hard" approach. Goals are focused on increasing value through profitability and cost-cutting efforts. GE's Jack Welch earned his nickname "Neutron Jack," during his earlier years when he focused on cost-cutting measures that improved profitability.

> **definition**
>
> **Theory E:**
> Economic value when changes are based on economic issues, such as shareholder value.
>
> **Theory O:**
> Organizational Capability when changes are developed over time, by focusing on the corporate culture and human capability of a firm.

Dimensions of Change	Theory E	Theory O	Theories E & O Combined
Goals	Maximize Shareholder return	Develop organizational capabilities	Embrace the differences of economic value and org. capability
Leadership	Manage change from the top down	Encourage participation from the bottom up	Set direction at the top, engage people below
Focus	Emphasize structure and systems	Build up corp. culture: behaviors and attitudes	Focus together with E-Systems & O-Culture
Process	Plan & establish programs	Experiment and evolve	Plan for spontaneity
Reward System	Motivate with financial incentives	Motivate by use of pay as fair exchange, thus building commitment	Use incentives to reinforce change but not to drive it
Use of Consultants	Analyze problems and shape solutions	Support mgmt. in shaping their own solutions	Expert resources who empower employees

Source: Harvard Business Review, May/June 2000 P137

Theory O changes are developed over time, by focusing on the corporate culture and human capability of a firm.

This "soft" approach to implementing change is a circular process, where individual and organizational learning evolves from making change, getting feedback, deliberating, and then making further changes. Jack Welch later became a business "guru" by establishing mentoring processes that allowed change and continuous improvement.

In a May/June 2000 *Harvard Business Review* article, *Cracking the Code of Change*, authors Michael Beer and Nitin Nohria described these theories in detail. Their chart (listed below) identifies six key elements to change, and how the theories relate to each element. The six elements are: *Goals, Leadership, Focus, Process, Reward Systems, and the use of Consultants.* The authors caution that it is very difficult and rare to combine both theories in the way Jack Welch did in his 20 years. This educational process in which you are now involved is about improving your chances. Remember that it took Welch 20 years to pull it off!

Organizational Transformation

Francis Gouillart and James Kelly of Gemini Consulting wrote *Transforming the Organization*. (McGraw-Hill, 1995) Many of the basics of this chapter relate directly to this CSI workbook. In short form, the CSI workbook is about "Reframing Corporate Direction, Restructuring the Company, Revitalizing the Enterprise, & Renewing People.

Organizational Transformation

"....*The orchestrated redesign of the genetic architecture of the corporation, achieved by working simultaneously, although at different speeds, along the four dimensions of Reframing, Restructuring, Revitalization, and Renewal*" (P. 7)

Reframing

Reframing refers to the company's ability to redefine its "Conventional Wisdom." It is about abandoning "We always do it this way." Successful reframing occurs when innovation, flexibility, and a new vision are instituted into the organization. There are three areas that control this dimension: **Vision, Mobilization, and Measurement Systems**.

Mobilization refers to the development of leaders. It involves the institutionalization of change agents, encourages the formation of Natural Work Teams throughout the organization, and develops Executive and/or Steering Committees or Teams. It is about building a groundswell of support. The foundation of teams, as you learned earlier, is to develop cross-functional as well as fresh insights of the business and its environment. It is about preparing people to accept change on a continuous basis. It is about having a system—teams—that will balance the company's needs for positive change with the individual's need for worth. Teams allow for interactive coaching and feedback.

TEAM TIP

The foundation of teams, as you learned earlier, is to develop cross-functional as well as fresh insights of the business and its environment.

Vision refers to the company's ability to form and implement a "Strategic Intent." Gouillart and Kelly refer to it as the "ultimate purpose, aspiration, and analytical diagnosis... (it must be) bold, broad, but not too broad, and looking a long way ahead." The process of developing the vision involves the allocation of resources, prioritization of expectations among constituencies or stakeholders, and establishing the organization's values that describes the company's "Non-negotiable" behaviors.

In Ken Blanchard and Sheldon Bowles' book, *GUNG HO!* they refer to values in the following way: "Goals are for the future. Values are *NOW*. Goals are set. Values are *LIVED*. Goals change. Values are rocks you can count on. Goals set people going. Values sustain the effort. Values become real only when you demonstrate them in the way you act and the way you insist others behave. In a 'Gung Ho' organization, values are the *REAL BOSS*."

Measurement Systems refers back to Chapter 6, where the process of developing top level targets, such as KPI's and Balanced Scorecards were discussed. In other words, the targets or measurements must connect all areas of the company from the bottom up. Isolated targets or measurements are not lasting. Effective targets are used to identify opportunities to continually improve.

Restructuring

Restructuring deals with the Corporate Body, the deployment of assets, and the alignment of Work Processes. There are three areas that influence this dimension: *Economic Models, Reconfiguration of the Physical Structure, and the Redesigning of the Work Architecture*.

Developing successful **Economic Models** requires the financial dissection of the company into discrete collections of businesses. This exercise can be both excruciating and insightful. Done correctly, a value chain is developed for each business, recognizing the economic value of the partitioned business. It is about allocating resources by activity, based on cost and service;

definition

Measurement systems: the process of developing top level targets, such as KPI's and Balanced Scorecards, where the targets or measurements must connect all areas of the company from the bottom up.

for example, breaking down a company's revenues by product line, service, or application. Attaching costs to each area can be complex, but will eventually provide "Information" rather than "Data" relating to how the company is performing.

A word of caution regarding the economic model process. In Eliyahu's book, *The Goal*, he refers to this process with much disdain. When the accounting department explains that a product line is "Not making a profit," do you stop producing or selling the product? He shares the story of how the company cannot drop a product line just because it doesn't make money, because the overhead is fixed—including direct labor. As a result, the losing product pays for incremental overhead. Our experience has shown that economic models, taken to extremes, can create a worse solution to the problem than not having the system at all. It can *Mislead*!

Outsourcing and Offshoring are the results of this effort. We have learned a great deal about control of quality versus control of the customer. When your products are commoditized because you lack capacity to develop new products or services, then outsourcing and offshoring are your best choices for reducing costs. If you are developing new products and services, you can redeploy your company's most valuable resource, its people, to address those challenges without outsourcing. Growing companies rarely pursue outsourcing unless it is as a competitive advantage.

Reconfiguring the Physical Structure refers to the formulation of operations and network strategy. Areas include the alignment of individual facilities and articulating a sourcing strategy involving suppliers, vendors, and distributors. For example, if you have two locations, how do they communicate and share parts and inventory? What competencies exist at each location? Finally, is each facility right-sized for its expected performance?

Redesigning the Work Architecture refers to the effort involved in fostering a complete alignment of individual processes. Gouillart and Kelly describe this

effort as "Learning Loops". Peter Senge's book, *The Fifth Discipline*, refers to "Systems Thinking". They both refer to the process of focusing on cause and effect relationships (remember the fishbone diagram?), and implementing change from the learning process of identifying the chief cause, not the symptom, of the problem.

Revitalization

Revitalization is about "Bringing new life into the organization." It is about growth. It refers to *how* the company relates to its environment. Three areas that control this dimension are **Information Technology**, **Invention of New Businesses**, and most importantly, looking at your business from the eyes of the customer, that is **Market Focus.**

Information Technology refers to the "central nervous system" of the company as it attempts to improve local efficiency. As mentioned earlier, there are three ways to cut costs effectively: employee training, procedural changes, and "robotics." Procedural changes and 'automating a function using technology' are direct applications to this topic. It directly relates to Bar Coding, Databasing, Internet processes, (i.e., E-commerce), EDI (Electronic Data Interchange), Alliances, CAD (Computer Aided Design), CAM (Computer Aided Manufacturing), and SFA (Sales Force Automation). Building strong networking capabilities improves efficiency as information speeds across boundaries. It increases *learning*! The leadership team should be identifying areas where new technological capabilities can be applied quickly and will become the greatest possible financial benefit.

Invention of New Businesses refers to the activities that foster cross-fertilization of a company's core competencies, building alliances and making acquisitions. What team-training programs are integrating members from non-related teams? What alliances are being established to cross-market products and services to new customer bases? What weaknesses can be "shored up" by acquiring another company or person?

Market Focus, or looking at your business from the eyes of the customer, requires information and response. There are three elements to developing market focus: *The development of value propositions, segmenting the customer base by benefits, and designing the value delivery system.* Value Propositions are descriptions of the benefits and prices charged from a customer's point of view. Gouillart and Kelly have three rules for developing good value propositions:

1. Find customers as far down the supply chain as possible in order to get the *real* value.

2. Work on *one* customer at a time so that real insight, not group summaries, are developed.

3. Listen to the customer, but do not rely on them to tell you what to do.

Market segmentation by benefits avoids the typical segmentation areas, such as geography, industry, products, or age group. Benefit segmentation refers to the process of refocusing on "making the customer's life better," than on "selling products and services." This is a major mindset change, since most organizations are caught up with sales numbers and quotas. In some cases, the transition is extremely tough, especially when there are no teams to implement the change.

Designing the value delivery system refers to the alignment of all systems, (i.e., technological, organizational, and distribution) with the company's set of value propositions.

Renewal

Renewal deals with the "Spirit" of the Company. It is the "People Side" of the business. It goes beyond the generic performance reward systems typically found in organizations. Renewal is about having work at a higher order of importance than with money. Renewal covers three areas: *Reward Systems, Building Individual Learning, and Developing the Organization.*

Reward Systems refers to the recognition of performance aligned with the company's goals and measurements. Paying for performance is broken down into four basic areas: Profit Sharing, Incentive Allotments, Salary Increases, and Executive Incentives. Rewards can go beyond the corporate boundaries to include customers, distributors, and suppliers. Rewards could also involve non-monetary awards, such as education, personal growth, and mentoring opportunities.

Building individual learning requires a commitment to individual learning. It involves the systemic process of improving an individual's critical skills, balancing corporate supply and demand skills, and creating mentor-guided, life-forming projects for high-caliber people.

Developing the organization involves the process of human interaction to create a sense of community. Historically, organizational structure models were formed using a functional, matrix, or Small Business Unit (SBU) concept. Each has its merits. **Functional** units, such as R&D (Bell Labs under AT&T) provide needed focus for its own performance. **SBU** units operate independently from each other, almost on a competitive level. Conglomerates, such as United Technologies of the 70s and 80s have fallen out of favor in the public stock arena. However, in the '90s, a new breed; for example, Tyco, used a **Matrix** structure to

TEAM TIP

The use of teams allows for the communication and education of the organization on a "Micro" level.

blend the independence of an SBU and the efficiency of the functional structure by cross-marketing and integrating each new acquisition.

The use of teams allows for the communication and education of the organization on a "Micro" level. The idea is to cultivate a company's large knowledge base by encouraging creativity, innovation, and entrepreneurship. Gouillart and Kelly recognize that "having a healthy sense of independence, self-reliance, and self-responsibility is the mark of a good team" when connected to a goal. If independence is a virtue, then being "connected" is a necessity. Effective teams are "connected," having developed a knowledge architectured management process combined with technology.

Knowledge Architecture and Knowledge Management Process refer to the systematic approach to learning and developing organizational knowledge. They are systemic approaches to collect, analyze, and communicate knowledge throughout the company. Your training to this point has been to meet the goal of creating this "System."

As you complete this chapter, be aware that you are in a global environment with an immediate focus on local issues. Your ability to recognize change and to adapt to change, especially global change, will allow your company to follow you and your team. Be ever so mindful of the old saying relating to how growing companies evolve: "It is permitted, unless forbidden." In maturing organizations, "it is forbidden, unless permitted." Trust builds with consistency, care, character, and competency. Teams have a way of building trust faster than any other means.

CHAPTER 8

THE BUSINESS
LIFE CYCLE

Learning Objective Questions from
Chapter 7: Implementing Change

🖊 *What are the Key elements of Theory "O"?*

🖊 *What are the Key elements of Theory "E"*

🖊 *What are the Key Element changes when you try to combine both?*

🖊 *Please name and describe the four dimensions of Organizational Change:*

🖊 *Please name and describe the four dimensions of Organizational Change:*

1)

2)

3)

4)

THE BUSINESS LIFE CYCLE

Introduction

Dr. Ichak Adizes developed a Business Life Cycle theory in the 1970s. His 1988 book, *Corporate Life Cycles: how and why corporations grow and die and what to do about it* is a compilation of several studies he performed while developing his theories. He defined problems into two basic forms: *Normal and Abnormal*.

Normal problems are those problems that are fairly predictable. They come and go as the organization passes from one life cycle stage to the other. Normal problems for growing companies can be described as follows: Poor Cash Flow, High Sales Growth, Conflicts with Strategic Direction, and Developing Rules to Improve Profitability. Normal problems are also challenges that do not require outside intervention to solve them.

Abnormal problems have two categories: Complexity and Pathology. An abnormal problem usually requires intervention by outside consultants because the organization does not have the ability, experience, or energy to solve them. *Complexity* represents those frequently found issues that hold the company hostage. For example, frequent change orders to a construction design or manufactured part adds complexity in the areas of scheduling, billing, costing, and customer relations. *Pathology* or *Pathological* problems are those issues that are not found frequently and continue to grow, regardless of management's attempts to correct them. For example, a company is growing rapidly, and the founder is retaining such tight control over the decision-making process that he/she becomes both the greatest asset and the greatest liability. This type of problem cannot be solved by an inside person, unless that person is willing to sacrifice his/her career at that company. If change and adaptation do not emerge in the organization, which usually impacts power centers and fiefdoms, the number and seriousness of the problems will grow exponentially.

Understanding the issues of each stage of the life cycle helps organizations develop a more effective diagnosis of their problems' causes and effects. In Chapter 4, we reviewed how to problem solve by first learning to identify the problem—by its causes, rather than by its symptoms. This chapter is about learning the predictable organization behaviors in order to improve the chances of corrective change.

Management Roles

As mentioned in Chapter 2, there are four (4) roles of management: "P," "A," "E," & "I." The "P" means **'Producer'** or performing results. An organization consisting of one person or many must produce desired results or nothing gets done. Goal setting, cold call selling efforts, or working overtime to make deadlines are all illustrative of management's "P" role.

The "A" or **Administrator** represents management's role in doing things "right" or efficiently. While the "P" was about getting the 'right things done,' the "A" wants 'things done right.' Organizations hire sales and production people to produce sales or products. They also hire for the Accounting, H/R, and Engineering departments to do something correctly. They make sure the invoices are correct, that people issues are managed, and the products developed are safe; and, they also meet customer expectations.

Both the "P" and the "A" are considered short-term roles. The short-term activities create faster results. For the "P," it is effectiveness. For the "A," it is efficiency. The long term management roles involve the "E" and the "I."

The "E" or **Entrepreneur** role encompasses the long-term ability to create change and innovation. It is this role, the long-term ability to create new products or services at lower cost and higher quality that enables the business to survive. How many times have you read or heard about a person who has developed 25 or more patents but has not been able to make and sell the ideas he/she has created? These types of "Pure" entrepreneurs are usually changing ideas and direction all the time. They are creative, work strange hours, and have a great disdain for rules and regulations that will affect their ideas. They are known for breaking "the rules." The concept of "E" is that it takes a very long time to create effective discovery and it requires a "nurturing" environment that will allow change to occur through experimentation.

The "I" stands for **Integration**. It can also mean "Interdependency." It is about management's values. Integration is about the organization's 'religion' or consciousness. It is about management's ability to be "team players;" building values and teamwork. Therefore, 'religion' is not something that can be developed quickly, but it evolves over time, and is longer lasting than the next customer found.

The P,A,E,I roles vary in strength and dominance throughout the various stages of the Life Cycle. As we go

Role	Function
(P)roducer	Effectiveness
(A)dminister	Efficiency
(E)ntrepreneur	Effectiveness
(I)ntegrate	Efficiency

through the Life Cycle stages, you will see how the roles evolve and change.

First Growth Stage:
Courtship

The courtship stage represents the founder's commitment to an idea. As with an early stage of a human mating ritual,

Cultures: PAEI

Source: "Corporate Lifecycles" - Ichak Adizes 1988

P=Production, A=Administration E=Entrepreneurism, I =Integration

Stable PAeI

Prime
PAEi

Adolescence
pAEi

Go-Go
PaEi

Infant
Paei

Courtship
paEi

Premature
Aging PAeI

Unfulfilled paEi
Entrepreneur

Founder/ P-E-
Family Trap

Infant P---
Mortality
Affair --E-

Aristocracy
pAeI

Early Bureacracy
pA-i

Bureacracy
-A--

Death

Growing | Aging

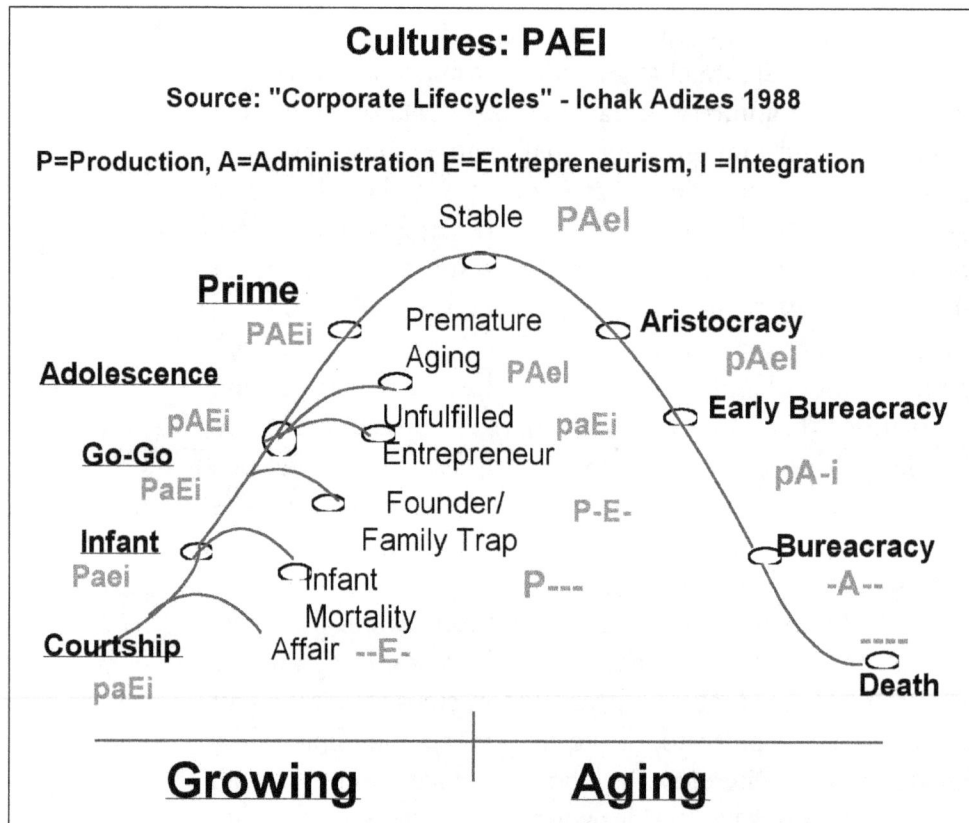

this stage involves excitement, lots of action and discovery, and getting positive feedback to go forward "together." However, if things don't go well and the entrepreneur begins to look at other opportunities, then the idea dies by "an affair" with another idea or "date." The founder's goal should be to satisfy a market need, and to create value added. The "E" becomes the dominant role, as creativity, innovation, and ability to change quickly to market needs drive the company forward. At this stage, risk begins to build as commitment to the idea overcomes the urge to find other ideas. As the founder develops more feedback that his idea will grow, a never ending cycle of effort and reward develops. The founder can become a "fanatic" about the business, which is healthy and normal at this stage, but abnormal in later stages. Team development, and piloting new products or programs evolve in the same way. Once the business evolves from the courtship stage, risks rise dramatically.

Second Growth Stage:
Infant

At this stage, there is a feverish pitch to produce results since the risks are much higher than ever before. The "baby" needs two things: love and food. The "love" comes from the founder's (or internal champion's) undying commitment to the business. Like a mother of a newborn, the founder must attend to the baby's never-ending "crying." Therefore, it is not always "fun," compared to when the founder was "dating." Finding new customers, paying the bills, hiring new employees, scheduling deliveries, and all sorts of other details are not things entrepreneurs enjoy, or desire to do for any length of time.

For the business to survive, the responsibility to produce is all on the shoulders of the founder, no one else. Therefore, the "P" becomes the dominant role, with the "E" taking a "back seat" to keep the business alive. The business needs food—that is money—or it will die of starvation. It is very common to hear of cash shortages and lots of action. There are no "systems" to hire people, pay bills, and so forth. As a result, the company displays inconsistent performance, management by crisis, poor delegation, and the creation of a situation that constantly tests the founder's commitment to the business.

Once the company finds its niche, and has the ability to create new customers consistently, the cash flow of the company stabilizes, and the risks of the founder begin to diminish. At this stage, the company emerges into the *Go-Go* stage. If the founder loses commitment or the company cannot create a positive cash flow, the ability of the company to survive begins to deteriorate. The lack of "love" or "food" kills the "baby."

Third Growth Stage:
Go-Go

At this point, the business is doing very well. The company is taking on more products and services to meet customer demand. It may be adding new locations, spending on

Research and Development (R&D), and the fun of the courtship stage begins to come back. The muted "E" comes back with a roar, with lots of ideas generating lots of opportunities. In fact, there are usually *too many* opportunities! There is lots of action, lots of ideas, and there are so many changes going on that no one knows for sure what is going on. But it is sure fun to be there!

If the founder begins to control the organization—not allowing delegation to occur—the business begins the process of aging. The founder's trap evolves when the founder does not give up control or does not institutionalize the "E," and his/her inner circle stifles the company, forcing the lower level entrepreneurs and producers to leave. Arrogance is a common description of this abnormal stage in the life cycle.

However, if the founder allows the development of delegation to occur, the organization begins a very rocky ride into adolescent stage.

Fourth Growth Stage
Adolescent

At this point, there's much excitement and lots of ideas that are not getting done or are poorly executed. Things aren't going "just right." The organization's character is like a teenager who hides beer in the bushes, wants new expensive clothes, or borrows mom's car without her permission. What happens in business is that individuals or groups will hide expenses, want the latest technology, or enter into agreements that nobody else knows about. In some cases, the firm's bank where the company borrows money may be asking for reports that indicate to them how well the company is performing. The banker may ask the owner to hire a CFO or Controller to help fix the problems. No matter what, these new people are hired, are needed, and are about to change the rules, *big time*.

Remember when you could submit expense vouchers without receipts? Not anymore. How about skipping employee reviews because you are too busy? Forget it.

How about selling a few more units to your favorite customer who is well over their credit limit, and has been slow paying, but is desperate for those units? *No Way!*

Everyone is about to face their worst nightmare—change. Change from the way things used to be done. Change from the fun of doing things without having controls over every decision made. At this stage, conflict arises, and that is normal. What is abnormal is when retaliation sets in, rather than cooperation.

If the CEO sides with his old buddies in Sales or Engineering, the changes are doomed, and the company slides in performance. If the CEO sides with the Controller, then many of his loyal followers may leave or threaten to leave. At this stage, it is more important to do things right than to do more things. Therefore the "P" becomes small while the "A" becomes large. You are learning how to use teams to make positive change in order to avoid either of the typical abnormal events from occurring. If you look at the Dell Computer company's sales figures since 1988, when it went public, it went through a short-2-year period where the Board of Directors intentionally SLOWED down the growth of the company to fix their operational performance, to focus on PROFITABLE growth. The following years of revenue growth also included historical profits as well.

Fifth Growth Stage
Prime

If the organization successfully enters into *Prime*, it will have revived the feelings of Go-Go as the Producers or "P" turn up the juices again. The "E" was never lost, instead, it was nurtured and controlled. Prime looks like a controlled 'Go-Go.' In Prime, the excitement and action of a *Go-Go* coupled with the execution of the Adolescent combines to produce great sales increases, along with excellent profit results. Common Prime Characteristics are:

- The company has functional systems and organizational structure,
- The founder's vision and creativity has been institutionalized,
- There is a results orientation, satisfying customer needs,
- Management makes plans and follows them,
- The company is predictable and excels in performance,
- The organization can afford growth in both sales and profits,
- The company creates new infants.

Microsoft in the Early 1990s is a good example of Prime. Bill was brash; sales were exploding; they were buying companies, and looking at all sorts of ideas and activities. They were making tons of money too. And then, arrogance set in.

First Aging Stage:
Stable

When arrogance sets in, the company's ability to create new ideas diminishes. Bill Gates wrote a book that expressed his view of the world in the 21st century and it did not include the Internet! It took two skunk works employees nearly three years to educate Bill and his team on the importance of the Internet. Bill's focus was on Windows.

But before that change occurred, every idea about the Internet was stifled and muted. Good people who felt that their internet ideas were going nowhere left the company. The "E's" were leaving. These idea-makers were starting companies that Microsoft would have to buy later. Stable companies begin losing the ability to create new infants that are long-term builders of equity.

Growing	Aging
• Personal success comes from taking risk	• Personal success comes from avoiding risk
• Expectations exceed results	• Results exceed expectations
• Cash poor	• Cash rich
• Emphasis is on function over form	• Emphasis on form over function
• Focus on what to do and why to do it	• Focus on how and who did it
• People are kept for contributions in spite of their personalities	• People are kept for • their personality not for their contribution
• "It is permitted unless forbidden"	• "It is forbidden, unless permitted"
• Problems are seen as opportunities	• Opportunities are seen as problems
• Sales & operations call the shots	• Corporate staff call the shots
• Political power is with sales dept.	• Political power with fin & admin
• Management controls the org.	• The organization controls mgmt
• Sales orientation	• Profit preoccupation
• Driven by value-added goals	• Driven by political gamesmanship
• Change in leadership changes org.	• Changes in systems changes org.
• Mgmt drives the momentum	• Mgmt is driven by inertia
• A person's responsibility is not matched with authority	• A person's authority is not matched with responsibility
• Consultants are needed	• Insultants are needed

Aging companies have these common characteristics:

- Lower expectations of growth,

- Suspicious of change,

- Focus is on past achievements, not future visions,

- Rewards those who do what they are told to do,

- More interested in interpersonal relationships, than in risk,

- Fewer expectations to conquer new markets, technologies, and frontiers.

Second Aging Stage:
Aristocracy

Because Microsoft was becoming a follower, rather than a leader, it was now forcing change in the marketplace by controlling price and distribution, rather than new products. In Aristocracy, the goal is *Return on Investment*, not sales and market share.

Why? Because their ability to grow has diminished, so they can only raise prices or control the sales channel to keep their profits up. If people don't make their numbers, they leave. Thus, those who survive have developed protection around them. It becomes more important to "Get along than to get things done."

As a result, this protection comes from relationships with the owners or key influentials, or these survivors have control over certain customers or technologies that cannot be replaced easily. Not only are the E's leaving in droves, but the company's ability to produce new sales is lost. In later stages, the company's sales start dropping and the later aging stages of Early Bureaucracy and Bureaucracy begin.

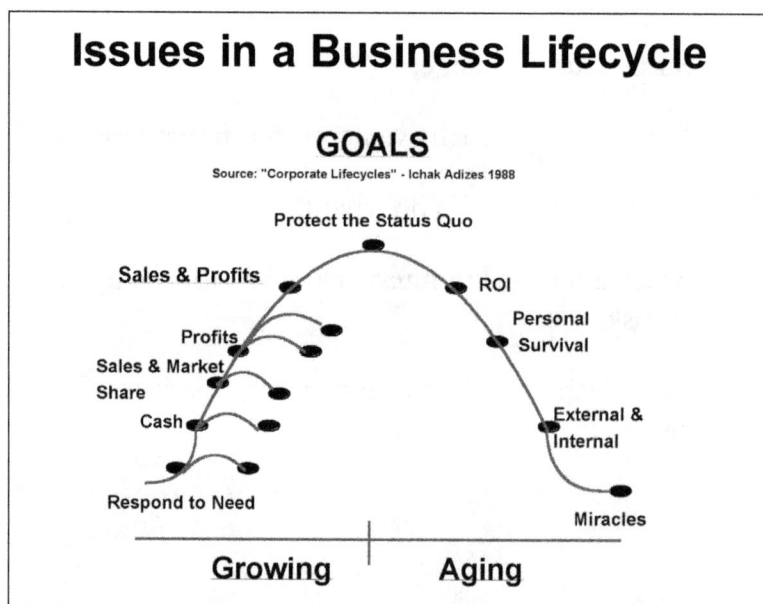

Issues in a Business Lifecycle

GOALS

Source: "Corporate Lifecycles" - Ichak Adizes 1988

Protect the Status Quo

Sales & Profits — ROI

Profits — Personal Survival

Sales & Market Share

Cash — External & Internal

Respond to Need — Miracles

Growing | **Aging**

Final Aging Stages:
Early Bureaucracy/Death

Now the company is facing a major crisis. The organization is best described as fiefdoms. People survive by politics, not by producing results. Thus, conflict arises in a similar fashion as in the Adolescent stage, only the problems are far worse. Profitability and customer relations are poor because of the finger-pointing as to *Who* rather that *What* caused the problems to surface.

In many late stage aging companies, the lower rung employees show up for work, just punching in, and not putting in any extra effort. They fear that they will lose their job for making a mistake. And new ideas are not permitted nor welcomed. So why bother helping?

In closing, as you assess your organization and the changes you want to make, be sure that you also recognize the cultural issues. Listed below are some cultural differences between a Growing and Aging Organization.

Growing vs Aging Quiz

Please select one statement from each numbered line that best illustrates your view of your organization, not of you individually. If you are the owner or president of a company, answer as a subordinate (and be honest).

1) Personal Success:	A) Our success comes from taking risks	
	B) Our success comes from avoiding risks	Circle One: A B
2) Forecasts & Plans:	A) Our goals and expectations exceed results	
	B) Our results exceed expectations	Circle One: A B
3) Finance:	A) We are cash poor	
	B) We are cash rich	Circle One: A B
4) Emphasis:	A) We want to do many things	
	B) We want to do things right	Circle One: A B
5) Dynamics:	A) We focus on what & why to do something	
	B) We focus on who and what to do	Circle One: A B
6) Contribution:	A) Results are more important that getting along	
	B) Getting along is valued more than results	Circle One: A B
7) Ideas & Change:	A) Everything is permitted, unless expressly forbidden	
	B) Everything is forbidden, unless permitted	Circle One: A B
8) Problems:	A) Problems are seen as opportunities	
	B) Opportunities are seen as problems	Circle One: A B
9) Political Power:	A) Marketing and Sales Dept. have "the power" over other depts	
	B) Finance, Acctg and/or Legal Depts have it	Circle One: A B
10) Decision Process:	A) Operating functions call the shots	
	B) Corporate staff call the shots	Circle One: A B
11) Responsibility:	A) Everyone knows who is boss, but not sure who is responsible for what	
	B) Responsibility is clear, Who's the Boss?	Circle One: A B
12) Management:	A) Management is in control of the organization	
	B) The "system" or organization is in control	Circle One: A B
13) Momentum:	A) Management drives the company towards success	
	B) We haven't been driving success in a long time	Circle One: A B
14) Leadership:	A) Changing the leader will change the organization	
	B) Changing the leader will not create big changes	Circle One: A B
15) Growth:	A) We are sales oriented	
	B) We are consumed with profit generation	Circle One: A B
16) Change Ability:	A) It would be fairly painless to change our organization & direction	
	B) It would be VERY painful for us to change	Circle One: A B
17) Goals:	A) Most of us focus on sales and/or profitability	
	B) Our focus is cash flow and/or personal survival	Circle One: A B

When done, please count the number of A's & B's: Total A's _____ Total B's _____

(Combining A&B totals should add up to 17)

CHAPTER 9

MANAGEMENT CONCEPTS

Learning Objective Questions from Chapter 8: The Business Life Cycle

✎ | *What are the four roles of management, and which represent effectiveness or efficiency?*

1)

2)

3)

4)

✎ | *What are the common traits of a company on the GROWING side of the life cycle?*

MANAGEMENT CONCEPTS

Introduction

This chapter was placed here to remind people what management is all about. Even the most educated managers can get lost with all of the latest books and management trends. The premise of this chapter is Peter Drucker's book, *The Practice of Management* (Harper Row, 1954). Why this book?

Over 100 years ago, very few people wrote about management. Frederick W. Taylor (1856-1915) created the term "Management Consultant" and assisted prominent manufacturing companies in the areas of operational efficiencies. He used time and motion studies that led to improved cycle times and less waste. Those time and motion studies were the early stages and processes that are now termed "Statistical Process Control."

The term "Manager" was first used in city government, when city managers became prominent. The first use of Management Principles was developed in 1901, for the US Army, by Teddy Roosevelt's Secretary of War, Elihu Root (1845-1937). By the time Drucker showed up in this world in 1909, much of the world's business models had changed rapidly. The corporate model had exploded, where single proprietorships like Ford Motor Company evolved from a single person dynasty into a complex organism.

What distinguished Drucker from Taylor was his focus on management, rather than operations. Where W. Edward Deming's quality focus using statistical control is based on the early studies of Taylor, it is the use of teams and other management concepts that are based on Drucker's book, *The Practice of Management*. "*Practice...*" was the first book of its kind to write about management and it became the foundation for a slew of current trend-setting management books.

The book introduces many "firsts." Drucker introduces the word **teams** as a process for CEO's to implement change and improve governance issues, applying team concepts to the Boards of Directors (p176-178). The term **Management by Objectives**, (or MBO) was also first coined in the book. In the '60s, MBO became a curse word as poorly trained managers used MBO for their own individual benefit. More importantly, Drucker outlines the use of benchmarks and goals that are the premise of *Theory E.*

The book also describes the basis of *Theory O*, where Drucker explains as his "manifesto", the use of the term "Human Organization" (P 289). He discusses the use of Integration (or integrating people), and motivating people by using more than money—by keeping people informed and having a managerial vision. Pretty crazy stuff for the 1950s.

Drucker first coined the term "Executive Team," relating the term to both the key managers and the board. It is Drucker, not others, who promoted the use of teams back in the 1940s and '50s. It is because of people like Deming, who rediscovered teams while working with the Japanese that the team vogue resurfaced.

Here is another point that Drucker is famous for: "Management has to learn how to do *new* things rather than to do the old things better" (Page 97). The competitive challenge or differentiator of the future will be *ideas*, not physical assets. This fundamental change is why you are now reading and doing homework. Not everyone is "getting it." People are still mismanaged and stifled, and organizations are consolidating because of this lack of knowledge. It is the foundation of why companies come and go.

What is the Purpose of a Business?

Before that question is answered, think about the possible answer. Is it "to make money?" Or how about "to produce a product?" Another popular answer is "to create employment opportunities." When we ask the audience during a speaking engagement, "What is the purpose of a business?," we get lots of different answers. Rarely do we get this answer: *"To Create Customers"*.

Why is "creating customers" the right answer? Let's take a look. In order to "make money" we need to have a customer pay us. In order to hire somebody, a customer has to need that person, and still pay us. And how many times have you heard of a product nobody wants? Ford's Edsel comes to mind. Is there a business in creating products that no one wants? Not in Drucker's mind. "Creating customers" is about *knowing* your customers' needs and wants.

If the purpose of a business is to "create customers", the purpose of management is to keep the business alive by allocating resources. Gary Hamel, co-author of *Competing for the Future* wrote that it *"used"* to be the function of management to allocate resources, but that has now evolved to *"Attracting"* resources. Why? Because innovation and implementation require scarce resources (skilled people and money), and the ability to attract those resources differentiates those companies that grow from those that don't. The function of profit, in Drucker's terms, is a measurement system of management performance. It is not *"The"* measurement system, but *"A"* measurement system.

A business needs to "create customers" in order to make products, hire people, and make money. But how do you create customers? Drucker writes that there are two ways, through **Marketing** and **Innovation**.

What is Marketing?

For those of you who have taken Marketing in school, you learned that there are the famous *five* P's: *Product, Price, Promotion, Place, and People.*

Nine Steps for a Successful Marketing Plan

Step 1: Prepare a Business Review. An overview of the company identifying the company's strengths, weaknesses, opportunities, and threats. It can also include Category Trends, Product Analysis, Behavior Trends, and a Competitive Analysis. In some cases, it also includes Target Market Assessments relating to Consumer or B2B (Business to Business) Segments, and Product Awareness.

Step 2: Develop Sales Objective. Setting both quantitative and qualitative objectives.

Step 3: Identifying New Target Markets. Understanding each market segment, primary and secondary markets, demographics, buying habits and then relating them to your sales objectives.

Step 4: Developing Positioning Statements. Comparing your product or service to the competition, listing the attributes of importance, and building an emotional relationship with the customer.

Step 5: Clarifying the Marketing Strategies. These are the execution strategies. Examples include: Build the market or steal it, Branding, Packaging, Pricing, Seasonality strategies, and Merchandising, to name a few.

Step 6: Articulate Communication Goals. Understanding the strategies to satisfy the 4 A's: Awareness, Attitude, and Action, repeat Action.

Step 7: Defining and Executing 4 of the 5 P's: Product/Branding/Packaging, Pricing, Place/Distribution, and Promotion/Events.

Step 8: Clarifying your Advertising Campaign. Define your objectives (audience, geography, seasonality, etc) and execution (forms of media: Radio, Print, etc.).

Step 9 Execute and Follow-up. Communicating the plan, developing lists, evaluation, and market research and testing.

Product relates to the product or service that the customer will pay for. **Price** stands for the value created by the product or service, and is the measure of its worth. **Promotion** is the description of the activities and investments made to improve customer awareness. **Place** represents the distribution channel and the processes that involve the development of the product or service to be used by a customer. And finally **People**, which relates to the function of understanding that customer needs are about *people*, and that the effort to sell is about understanding *people*.

Marketing is a science all by itself. Building a marketing plan can be very complex and extensive. The table on the previous page outlines some of the common steps and the issues relating to building a comprehensive marketing plan.

> **definition**
>
> *Place:*
> represents the distribution channel and the processes that involve the development of the product or service to be used by a customer.

Innovation

Innovation is about creativity. It is about an organization's ability to create new ideas, new products or services, or to make change in processes, strategies, or other related areas. Encouraging Innovation in a growing or complex organization can be very difficult if the organization's *trust* among the members is not fully developed nor understood. We discuss trust in later chapters. Additionally, innovators or "entrepreneurs" are usually abrasive or demanding, leaving those who are more integrative to place these people in low regard.

What Business are We In?

Drucker wrote: "That the question is so rarely asked, at least in a clear and sharp form, and so rarely given adequate study and thought is perhaps the most important single cause of business failure."

From Drucker's point of view, the first question to ask is "*Who is the Customer.*" As we have already discussed how to establish that in Chapter 5, the basic process of surveying customers. But it goes beyond surveys. Who are these people? And yes, even though the invoice may have a corporate name, Britt Beemer says 95% of all sales are driven by people, not items or processes. The key here is to understand the demographics of the customer.

From that question comes "How does the customer buy?" This question usually refers to the process of the transaction. Are you a retail store that people come into by advertising? Are you a wholesaler who requires people to generate relationships that drive sales? Knowing the demographics of your customer allows the discussion to drift into a variety of tactical moves to improve or innovate the process.

Intuitively, most successful entrepreneurs figure these two questions out, but never share the answers with others. A key issue with the team process is to know these two items first before going further. Which then leads to the big question: "What does the customer buy?" Obviously, this discussion leads to products and services. But why here? Many ask "shouldn't this be first?" If you own a gold mine, do you need to know who the customer is? Are you going to sell 50 lb ingots of gold in a grocery store? What is the consumer going to do with these ingots once they are carried home? How do you ship these ingots? Who will store them, and ship them? Now, let's change the mine to copper or aluminum. Ask the same questions. How about a petroleum refiner or a farmer? The product isn't as important as the customer and the process.

We conclude the questions with "What does the customer look for when considering Value?" At this point, you have a lot of knowledge about the customer, how the buying process works, and what products they are looking for to fit their needs; now it comes down to "value." Our intention is not to cover basic economic concepts, such as "exchanges." It is important that we do not get stuck on *price* issues. We do want to know what characteristics create value, such as time of delivery, product features, intrinsic savings, and benefits.

The challenge then becomes, "What *will* our business be?" Or better yet, "What *should* our business be?" What are the market trends? Describe the market in terms of 5, 10, and 15 years out. What will change the market structure? What

technologies are driving change? We are all witnessing the emergence of the internet.

One hundred years ago, our ancestors witnessed the development of electricity and use of oil. What good is electricity without a light bulb or telephone? Bill Hewlett and David Packard formed their company in 1937 to manufacture innovations in the electronic field? They did not focus on products until *after* they figured out who they were.

What good is oil without cars, planes, and petrochemical plants that produce plastics? A great exercise is to pretend you are back 100 years ago, and try to figure out what new industries will develop. TV's produced in the 1960s had vacuum tubes, not transistors in the production line. Did they replace radios? Not really. Neither have CD players. So, what business are you in?

Management Practices

Drucker identified five areas or practices to insure a strong "esprit de corps." They are:

1. Performance requirements must be high, with low tolerance for mediocrity, and rewards based on performance. The key here is accountability.

2. A job at every level must be rewarding in itself, not just a step up the ladder.

3. A rational and just promotion system. There must be opportunities to grow in role and responsibility.

4. A clearly defined "Management Charter" that spells out the decision process, who is accountable for what, and the rewards for success.

5. Management Integrity is not developed over time; it is already there and being used. Do not expect someone to change if they are unethical or lack integrity.

Management Development

Now that you have figured out what the future of the business will be, you have to focus on the management needs—to develop your future leaders and innovators. There are two basic principles: 1) it involves the entire management group; and 2) the process is dynamic, always focusing on the needs of tomorrow.

Job rotation is a methodology where specialists move from their primary function to other areas to broaden their skills and knowledge. The process of using teams allows the exchange of information to educate, without the risk of moving a successful person in, say engineering, and have them manage the accounting department.

The key to management development is to make sure you follow the five principles on the previous page.

Decision Analysis

What drives the structure of the organization is the PROCESS OF DECISIONS. The role of the CEO, the Board of Directors, and the shop floor manager are determined by the decisions they make. As Drucker put it, "it is no accident that the greatest single cause for failure of businesses to consolidate their growth, or for their relapse into smallness if not into bankruptcy, is the failure of the boss to give up making decisions when they are no longer his or hers to make."

There are four basic characteristics of a decision:

1. The Degree of Futurity. Does the decision commit the company to a long term contract, or does it affect a sales transaction?

2. The Scope of Impact. Does the decision affect one department or many?

3. Frequency. How often does a particular decision have to be made? Is it a rare decision? Then it must be carefully thought through from beginning to end. Is it a frequent decision? Then how far down should that decision be made?

4. Character or Values. Does it involve conduct, social/political beliefs, or ethical values? Decisions that challenge the organization's values require a higher level of authority.

Drucker reminds us that "Management is not concerned with knowledge for its own sake, it is concerned with performance." Delegating Decisions as well as authority improve performance.

New Millennium Challenges

In a book written nearly a half a century later, Drucker finishes off the 20th century with his book *Management Challenges for the 21st Century*. As he reviewed the historical aspects of management, he identified several key elements of change that are now taking place.

Knowledge workers are evolving from the role of subordinate employee to what could be termed "volunteers." Knowledge workers have mobility, desire satisfaction from their work, they need a challenge to stay put. Developing very clear mission and vision statements becomes a primary tool to keep and retain people. As a result, managing people is evolving into a "marketing job." The task is to lead people, and the goal is to improve the productivity by developing each person's strengths and knowledge. It must be a system that *attracts* people.

"Management exists for the sake of the institution's results. It has to start with intended results, and has to organize the resources of the institution, whether business, church, university, or a battered women's shelter, capable of producing results outside of itself."

People cannot manage change. To survive, people have to be adaptable to change. Drucker determined that in times of rapid change, distribution channels and its distributors change faster than other areas. Management must pay very close attention to their channels if they are to survive.

When implementing change, it was very important to Drucker that projects be "piloted" or implemented in small or isolated areas first, to prove sustainability. Once the piloted project was successfully completed, it could then be rolled out to the entire organization.

Change Leaders are those individuals or organizations that focus on opportunities, while developing systems to rapidly reduce the number of problems. What are the opportunities?

- Process needs

- Market or industry structural changes

- Customer demographic changes

- Perception or meaning changes

- Unexpected successes or failures by the organization or its competitors

- Gaps between customers and market processes, structure, or channels.

- New knowledge

In order to implement these changes, there are two types of budgets that Change Leaders use: Present Business and Future Business. **Present Business** Budgets are those revenues and expenditures that make up around 85- 90% of all expenses. The key characteristic of these budgeted items is the frequent changes to them. The remaining 10-15% of expenses is covered under **Future Business** expenditures, which have the characteristic of not changing in good times or bad. If the purpose of management is to keep the business alive by attracting and allocating resources, the future budget is a primary tool that allows the business to stay alive.

Management exists because problems exist that are solved by people. Growth (or success) is usually the cause of the problems. Typical problem areas of growth include cash flow (rapid sales causes inventory and A/R growth), price stability (possible price wars), quality control, distribution and delivery, and management decision making. As the number of transactions increases, the likelihood is that more problems will surface.

In conclusion, one role of management is to solve problems. The process of teams is to improve the organization's ability to solve problems faster and with better outcomes. Your ability to "solve problems" and to have a system to support you is the focus and reason of why you have been sitting in the classes and working your way through this CSI workbook. We are almost finished with this stage of your education.

definition

Present Business budgets: those revenues and expenditures that make up around 85-90% of all expenses.

CHAPTER 10

THE MANAGEMENT PROCESS

Learning Objective Questions from Chapter 9: Management Concepts

✎ | What is the purpose of a business?

✎ | What is the purpose of management?

✎ | What are the five management practices explained by Dr. Drucker?

✎ | What/Who are "Change Leaders?"

✎ | What the the opportunities Change Leaders focus on?

✎ | Management exists because.....?

THE MANAGEMENT PROCESS

Introduction

Building a comprehensive strategic plan is very time consuming and complex in nature. Understanding the management process helps clarify certain elements of the Strategic Plan, and how to go forward with implementing that plan.

Dr Gerry Faust and Will Phillips developed a process over the years that identifies the key elements of the management process. It is called the "Executive Insight Process" or "EI." As the teams evolve into developing their ability to solve problems more effectively, the ability of the management team to quickly correct problems in order to focus on opportunities will improve. This CSI workbook prepares you for that process.

The "EI" Process

But what is the "EI" Process? It is a highly effective method to help identify the organization's strengths, weaknesses, opportunities, and threats in a very subtle and confidential, but effective way. The primary purpose of the EI process is to gather together the key people of an organization, to identify the top 10 problems of the business, and to then conclude with action plans for the top three problems for teams to solve.

There are five basic components to the EI Process: 1) The External Factors, 2) The Results, 3) The Culture, 4) The Strategic Factors, and 5) The Subsystem or Operational factors.

External Factors

The external factors relate to those issues that are generally affecting the organization from the outside. These areas could include competition, industry trends, or government regulation. In some cases, it could be the market's characteristics, such as farming or certain retail businesses, since they are seasonal in nature.

External factors could include the parent organization where a division is reactive to changes in the parent company's direction. Sometimes, a key determination of the severity to external factors comes from the industry itself, because it may not be growing or alternatively, demand for the products are waning. In some cases, barriers to entry issues also affect external factors.

A "barrier to entry" is a characteristic that keeps competition away. Franchising laws for auto dealers or fast food outlets are examples of "barriers to entry." Other barriers to entry include "scale" or size of the companies involved, like automobile manufacturing, or diverse retail such as Walmart or Sears. Having the only hardware store or gasoline station in the area can also be a barrier, because town ordinances may not permit any more of those types of stores. Patents and trademarks are also barriers to entry.

> **definition**
>
> **Barrier to Entry:** a characteristic that keeps competition away, franchising laws for auto dealers, for example.

The Results

The results involve those characteristics that best describe the outcomes of the remaining areas' performance. Profitability or customer satisfaction are two primary areas that are results. You cannot, all of a sudden, make a company profitable or a customer happy unless you change something.

Some additional areas that indicate the level of performance in the results area include:

- Market Share
- Company Growth
- Employee/Management Morale

- Absenteeism
- Employee/Management Turnover
- Successful Projects
- Consistency with Performance
- Meeting Goals, Deadlines, and Objectives
- Ownership Satisfaction
- Community Satisfaction

Culture

The Culture of an organization comprises both organizational values and disposition. It is the grease that allows the strategic and subsystem elements to produce good results. Key topics include:

- Optimism
- Proactive vs. reactive
- Signs of bureaucracy
- Goals that are stretchable and have management commitment
- Results orientation
- Dealing with difficult issues and conflict
- Ability to deal with risk, change, and creative people
- Teamwork and mutual respect

Strategic Elements

The Strategic elements refer to issues that affect the direction and values of the organization. Items that are covered in this area are:

Purpose and Direction
- Leadership
- Planning/Priorities
- Organizational Focus
- Philosophy/Orientation
- Communication

Structure and Delegation
- Job Clarity
- Delegation
- Employee/ Mgmt Involvement
- Organizational Structure

Information and Control
- Effective Meetings
- Communication of Information
- Effective Information
- Accountability
- Idea Development

Rewards and Recognition
- Incentive Systems
- Recognition

Subsystem/Operational Elements

These are the elements that affect the performance and execution of the organization. Where the strategic elements cover direction and values, the subsystem elements produce results. In fact, these items should be the operating priorities that are addressed in an annual business plan. These should be done by department or functional team. The subsystem or operational elements are categorized as follows:

Customer Needs
- Market Information
- Market Driven Changes
- Customer Service
- Product Line
- Market/Product Position
- Pricing
- Promotion
- Distribution
- Sales Staff

Product/Service Transformation
- Suppliers
- Facilities
- Research and Development
- Equipment and Maintenance
- Systems
- Workflow
- Inventory
- Quality Control
- Office Procedures
- Safety & Security

People
- Hiring
- Training
- Career Management
- Performance & Evaluation
- H/R Function
- Quality & Allocation of People

Money
- Cash Management
- Accounting Procedures
- Budgets
- Financial Management
- Accounts Payable

The intention of sharing the above items with you is to give you the breadth of the process as to how many issues it is able to identify within an organization. From these items, action plans will be developed that teams will need to address. In the event the EI process is not completed, the teams should identify the key issues from each area bulleted, and begin prioritizing these items for solving. Many times, it is very hard to clarify the key issues of each area in clearly defined terms. The key to improved performance is to identify those issues to solve and to bring those new issues to the surface on a scheduled annual basis.

Building a Strategic Plan

Strategic planning evolved over the years from a basic retreat of key executives to a more formal, institutional process for large corporations. The premise is to *plan*, rather than to *react* to market changes. The process starts with directional statements. There are six basic statements:

Vision: The view of the future, answering "What do you want to do?"

Mission: The organization's purpose, answering "Why you exist, or how do you want to get there?"

Business Definition: The boundaries of the business, such as markets, customers, products, services, geography, technology, and distribution.

Competitive Advantages: Identifying the key customer needs where you exceed the competition.

Core Competencies: The organization's abilities and skills. We will discuss these further on in the CSI workbook.

Values and Beliefs: The handful of values and beliefs that govern the organization's behavior.

Strategic Plan: 14 Steps

1. **Develop Market Intelligence:** Carefully analyze your customers, competition, and trends.

2. **S.W.O.T-Strengths, Weaknesses, Opportunities, and Threats.** The key is *knowing* those elements based on the strategic and subsystem elements described earlier in this chapter.

3. **Identify Your Core Competencies:** Later in this chapter, we will discuss the identification and development of the organization's core competencies.

4. **Develop Outside Industry Analysis**: by understanding how other unrelated industries apply their skills to improve performance and market penetration.

5. **Develop Trend Analysis, Future Views, and Mental Models**: We find that many strategic plans do not work with good data and clear views of where the company should be in the future. At this point, a mission and vision statement should be developed.

6. **Build Positioning Statements (5-15 yrs):** Positioning statements are discussed on the next page.

7. **Develop a Forecasting Model (1-5 Yrs):** A business plan should be incorporated within a strategic plan. A business plan forecasts out up to five years of financial statement, in order to insure proper capital investment.

8. **Develop Consensus on Purpose and Direction:** Once the plan is developed, "buy-in" needs to be gained, in order for any success to develop. No "Buy-in" means no success.

9. **Clarify Structure and Delegation and Mgmt Succession Issues:** Is the management team and the organization properly structured to implement at this time? Should roles and responsibilities change, in order to improve focus? Do you need to hire someone with those skills or experience that the firm lacks?

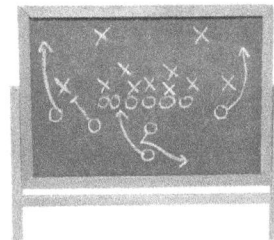

10. **Create Action Plans, Measurements, and Benchmarks:** It is very important to "pilot" small projects and problem-solving processes, then move into two *big* projects or issues that haven't been solved.

11. **Develop Rewards and Recognition:** Only at this point, can you begin to develop rewards and recognition (R&R) processes. If an organization develops R&R earlier than this 11th step, it is risking a great deal of healthy emotion and good will that may vaporize when tested. Make sure you have your measurements well defined before you start rewarding people.

12. **Develop Management Training and Education Problem Solving:** The future success of your organization rests on your fellow employees' abilities to solve problems. It requires a system and commitment to insure individual and team development.

13. **Execute Teams and Action Plans:** "Execute" does not mean to tie them to a post and shoot them, it means to empower them to make change and encourage risk taking as well as completion of tasks.

14. **Annual Review:** To avoid the common mistake of "projects started, but never finished," begin framing the foundations of success with monthly scheduled reviews, coupled by an annual review that assesses success and failure, strengths and weaknesses, and that develops action plans for the upcoming period. Be mindful that it is *not* about "who and how," but rather that it is about "what and why."

Strategic Positioning

Strategic Positioning is about your organization's intended direction when competing in the marketplace. Football teams develop players to compete in their own division, not in the whole league, because they play all of their division opponents twice in a season. They select special team players, linemen, and defenses to earn a spot in the playoffs.

The process of Strategic Positioning is much the same. The key is to get into the playoffs in order to get into the Superbowl. It is about "first things, first." Identifying how your division is preparing to play is your first step to winning the division. The second part is getting the right players prepared to win.

Arnoldo Hax & Dean Wilde wrote an article in Sloan Management Review, Winter 1999. *The Delta Model: Adaptive Management for a Changing World* described several key views of strategic positioning. The following section will review those premises developed by Hax and Wilde.

Three Points of the Delta Model: *Strategic Options*

Hax and Wilde developed a three point triangle or "Delta" symbol to identify the market positions of several public companies as they competed in their respective "divisions." The three options or positions are:

Best Product: Based on the well-known competitive approaches of price/low cost, or product differentiation. The **Low cost** approach is developed by achieving economies of scale, large market share, and simplifying processes or products. **Differentiation** relates to how a product/service differs in the marketplace with increased customer value using technology, branding, and special features. Walmart represents a typical example of this option; they market themselves as "lowest price, always." They invested heavily in technology in the mid 1980s that allowed them to compete against and displace Kmart as the lowest price retail store.

Customer Solutions: This option is driven by the focus on customer economics, not on the product's. In this position, a company develops very close relationships with its customers, understanding their needs, and then providing numerous, broad products, and services to fill those needs. In many cases, partnerships or alliances are formed to help fill those needs. The company EDI comes to mind because they focus on a company's needs and provide information technology services and products to win customers.

System Lock-in: The basis of this option is to develop standards or barriers to entry by attracting or developing relationships with "complimentors" who will enhance the company's product value. Microsoft comes to mind because they focused on having software developers to design their software using windows and their office suite.

Although a company may have various blends of these three options, we will focus on each separately in order to gain further insight.

Three Adaptive Processes

Hammer and Champy, who wrote the book *Reengineering the Corporation* in 1993, explained that companies should be viewed as processes rather than in terms of product, divisions, or functions. Hax and Wilde identified three processes that enabled companies to adapt to their respective marketplaces competitively. These three "Adaptive Processes" are:

Operational Effectiveness: These are the processes that involve the supply chain elements to produce and deliver to the customer. It usually relates to costs and infrastructure or capacity and efficiency.

Customer Targeting: These are the relationship-building activities that will identify, attract, satisfy, and retain customers by demonstrating improved revenue or lower costs to the customer.

Strategic Positioning

Best Product

Strategic Position

Customer Solutions

System Lock-In

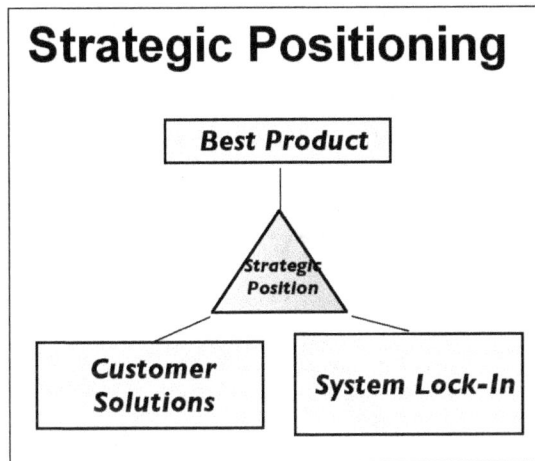

Source: Sloan Mgmt Review - Winter 1998.

Innovation: The ability to develop new or improved products or services through internal creativity and/ or marketing, technical, or process capabilities.

The Strategic Position chart illustrates the relationships between the adaptive processes and the three positions.

Nurturing Experimentation

Every organization has a conflict regarding the high cost of creating new products or services with the use of experimentation. A major development project could require thousands of experiments, in order to solve the problems inherent with the idea. New technologies are making it easier to experiment quickly and at far less cost. Methodologies, such as rapid prototyping, computer simulation, and internet cookies allow for faster and less costly feedback for an idea or experiment.

Stefan Thomke identified four characteristics that enable experimentation to link with learning:

1. Organize for rapid experimentation by using small development groups, running experiments in parallel instead of sequentially, and replacing old entrenched routines.

2. Fail early and often, but avoid mistakes. Experiments begin with clear objectives and expectations. Mistakes occur when loss of control of the project results in no learning.

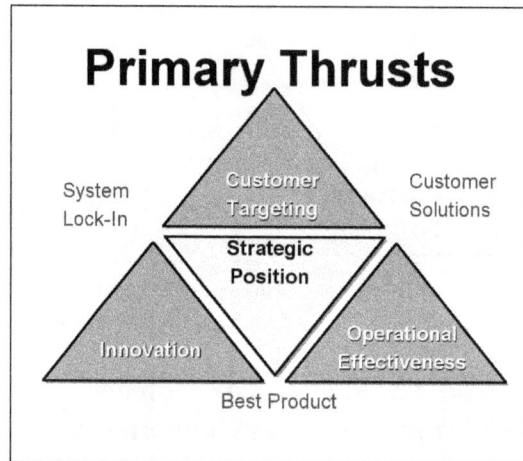

3. Anticipate and exploit early information. Identify upstream problems from the current issues. Balance the cost for the value by recognizing that higher cost variables may enhance the product later in the experiment, but not in the early stages.

4. Combine new with traditional technologies. One cannot assume that a new technology will replace an old one. In many cases, they will work better together than by working independently.

Understanding Core Competencies

Gary Hamel and CK Prahalad wrote *Competing for the Future* in 1994. The premise for their book was that "Top management's primary task is reinventing industries and regenerating strategy, not reengineering processes." They coined the phrase "Core Competency" as a strategic intent. Their view of a core competency was "a bundle of skills and technologies, rather than a single discrete skill or technology," to benefit customers.

	Best Product	Customer Solutions	System Lock-In
Operational Effectiveness	Best Product Cost • Identify Product Cost Drivers • Improve Stand-alone Product Costs	Best Customer Value • Improve Customer's Economics • Improve linkages across components for a "total solution"	Best Customer Value • Improve System Performance • Integrate products/services that enhance your product's value (Complimentors)
Customer Targeting	Target Distribution Channels • Maximize coverage through many channels • Obtain low cost distribution • Optimize sales channel mix and profitability	Target Customer Bundles • Enhance Customer interfaces • Explore Alliances to Bundle solutions • Select and develop key vertical market relationships • Examine sales channel ownership options	Target System Architecture • Identify leading complimentors in the system • Enhance complimentor interfaces • Harmonize system architecture • Expand number and variety of complimentors

Innovation	Product Innovation
	• Develop family of products based on common or simplified platform
	• First to Market, or follow rapidly a stream of products
		Customer Sourced Innovation
		• Identify and exploit joint development that links together the customer value chain
		• Expand offering into Cust. value chain to improve Cust. economics
		• Integrate and innovate customer care functions
		• Increase customer lock-in by customization and learning
			System Innovation
			• Emphasize features and supporting lock-in
			• Proliferate complimentors
			• Design proprietary standards within open architecture
			  ✓ Complex interfaces
			  ✓ Rapid Evolution
			  ✓ Backward Capability

Source: Competing for the Future by G. Hamil and C. K. Prahalad.

To create a future company, they identified three areas of strategy:

1. Change the "Rules of Engagement", like Charles Schwab did in the brokerage business.

2. Redraw the Boundaries between industries, like AOL and Time-Warner did in the late '90s.

3. Create entire new industries, like Apple did in the late '70s.

In all cases, it was about a commitment to creating a new class of customer benefits, rather than a specific opportunity with products or markets. It then becomes a management requirement to measure the changes in competencies, in order to know if they are eroding or strengthening. The internet is changing many companies' perception of the market and competencies.

The authors also identified eight ways to protect and defend your organization's Core Competencies:

1. develop a process for identifying core competencies,

2. develop a strategic architecture that includes setting acquisition goals for needed competencies,

3. prepare a clear set of priorities that define corporate growth and new business development,

4. develop accountability that maintains the first three items,

5. allocate resources for competency development,

6. measure and benchmark efforts against competition,

7. regularly review the organization's portfolio of competencies2

8. develop a team within the organization that will infect other areas or departments with their newly developed competencies.

The authors prepared a chart that will help in understanding how their view of strategic planning—integrated with core competency development—is different. The chart following here is from their book.

Developing Leaders

John Maxwell's book, *The 21 Irrefutable Laws of Leadership*, outlines several basic rules of leadership.

The laws are as follows:

1. **The Law of the Lid:** "Leadership ability is always the lid on personal and organizational effectiveness. If leadership is strong, the lid is high. If not, then the organization is limited".

2. **The Law of Influence:** Being a leader is not a "given." Having a position of authority, knowledge, or privilege will not create movement as in the same way having the influence or power to align people to your mission."

3. **The Law of Process:** There are four phases of leadership growth:
   1) if you do not recognize what you don't know, you will not grow,

   2) now that you recognize what you don't know, you can now begin to learn what you need to know, by developing actions or disciplines to improve oneself. "Leadership is developed daily, not in a day,"

   3) as your circle of influence expands, your effectiveness rises. People will remark how your knowledge has grown,

   4) as years, rather than weeks pass, your ability to influence will be continually engaged, requiring less effort. If you push too fast, you will miss a lesson or two that will be needed in future years.

> **definition**
>
> *Core Competency:* a bundle of skills and technologies, rather than a single discrete skill or technology to benefit customers.

	Strategic Planning	Strategic Architecture
Planning Goal	• Incremental improvement in market share and position	• Rewriting industry rules and creating new competitive space
Planning Process	• Formulaic and ritualistic • Existing industry and market structure as the base line • Industry structure analysis, (i.e., cost structure, value chain, segmentation, competitive bench marking) • Tests for fit between resources and plans • Capital budgets and resource allocation among competing projects • Individual businesses as the unit of analysis	• Exploratory and open-ended • An understanding of discontinuities and competencies as the base line • A search for new functionalities or new ways of delivering traditional functionalities • Enlarging opportunity horizons • Tests for significance and timeliness of new opportunities • Development of plans for competence acquisition and migration • Development of opportunity approach plans • The entire company as the unit of analysis
Planning Resources	• Business unit executives • Few experts • Staff driven	• Many managers • The collective wisdom of the company • Line and staff driven

4. **The Law of Navigation:** Good navigators "examine the conditions before making commitments, make sure their conclusions represent both faith and fact, and they listen to what others have to say."

5. **The Law of E.F. Hutton:** The old advertising campaign "When E.F. Hutton speaks, people listen" indicates several things about a leader's strengths: Character, Relationships, Knowledge, Intuition, Experience, Past Success, and Ability.

6. **The Law of Solid Ground:** Trust is the foundation of leadership. We discuss this subject in more length in Chapter 11: Personal Development.

7. **The Law of Respect:** In a new environment with a bunch of leaders, the group quickly identifies the stronger leaders and aligns to them. Good leaders respect stronger leaders.

8. **The Law of Intuition:** Because strong leadership is developed over time, a leader must develop intuition from experience and information, not from guesswork. Good leaders are accurate readers of their situation, trends, their resources, other people, and themselves. There are three levels:

    1) Those who naturally see it,

    2) those who are nurtured to see it, and

    3) those who will never see it.

Our research of talking to CEO's who have developed future CEO's for other companies have indicated that those who arrive at the top and stay there have done so because they have developed cross functional experiences that allow them to be comfortable with decision-making during ambiguous times. Some would call that "intuition", while we know that their "gut" has developed by their own experience as a leader, which was developed during risky exercises or activities surrounded with ambiguity.

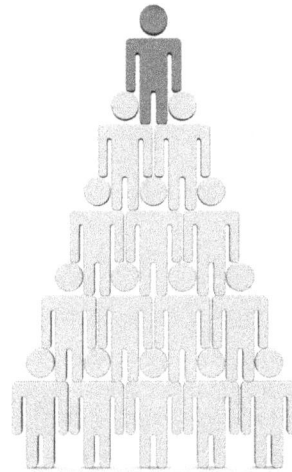

9. **The Law of Magnetism:** If you think that the people you attract could be better, then it's time for you to improve yourself.

10. **The Law of Connection:** A key to connecting with people is recognizing that even in a group, you have to relate to people as individuals. Leaders show how much they care before they show how much they know.

11. **The Law of the Inner Circle:** A leader's potential is determined by those people closest to him/her. There are five types of people a leader needs for success:

1) those who will motivate themselves,

2) those who will raise the morale in the organization,

3) those who will support and raise up the leader,

4) those who will raise up others, and

5) those who will raise up people who raise up other people.

12. **The Law of Empowerment:** The ability to find other leaders, build them up, give them resources, authority, and responsibility, and then turn them loose with purpose and direction. Your use of teams is to develop future leaders. Your challenge is to create an environment where future leaders can be developed without fear or retribution.

13. **The Law of Reproduction:** "We teach what we know, we reproduce what we are." Teams have a way to help mentor the next generation.

14. **The Law of Buy-In:** Leaders find the dream, and then find the people. People find the leader, and then find the dream. Or said differently, People will not follow worthy causes first, but they will be attracted to worthy leaders who promote worthwhile causes.

15. **The Law of Victory:** Leaders focus their attention on the team that is winning or achieving their goals. There are three components of victory:

1) Unity of vision,

2) Diversity of skills, and

3) a Leader dedicated to victory and raising players to their potential.

16. **The Law of Big MO:** Momentum is a leader's best friend. The key to improving momentum is to be prepared and motivated. By continually improving yourself, and learning to motivate yourself, a leader will create the right set of vibrations that will continually improve their effectiveness.

17. **The Law of Priorities:** Good leaders understand the three "R's:" what is *required*, what gives the greatest *return*, and what brings the greatest *reward*.

18. **The Law of Sacrifice:** Sacrifice is an ongoing process, not a one-time payment. Therefore, the higher up you are as a leader, the more sacrifice is expected—usually time.

19. **The Law of Timing:** There are four outcomes with timing:

   1) the wrong action at the wrong time leads to disaster,

   2) the right action at the wrong time brings resistance,

   3) the wrong action at the right time is a mistake;

   4) the right action at the right time is success.

20. **The Law of Explosive Growth:** To create early stages of growth, leaders lead followers. As the growth explodes, leaders lead leaders.

21. **The Law of Legacy:** There are four legacy principles:

   1) lead with a long-term view,

   2) create a leadership culture,

3) value team leadership above individual leadership,

4) pay the price today to assure success tomorrow.

Jack Welch Speaks About Leadership

In a Businessweek (1/30/06 P120) article, Jack responded to the question: **"I've been appointed to a senior leadership position for the first time... I want your advice on how to approach my new role."**

His response: "First of all, kudos are in order. Not for getting promoted, though that's great. But kudos because you seem to understand that being a leader means you really have to change how you act.... Before you are a leader, success is all about you. It's about your performance. Your contributions. When you become a leader, success is all about growing others. It's about making the people who work for you smarter, bigger, and bolder. Nothing you do anymore as an individual matters except how you nurture and support your team, and help its members increase their self-confidence.... Your success as a leader will come not from what you do, but from the reflected glory of your team."

Jack's advice to about how to make the transition to a leader:

1) "Actively mentor your people. Exude positive energy about life and the work you are doing together, show optimism about the future, and care."

2) "Care passionately about each person's progress. Give people feedback, not just at year-end and midyear performance reviews, but after meetings, presentations, or visits to clients."

3) "Make every event a teaching moment. Discuss what you like about what they are doing, and ways that they can improve."

4) "Your energy will energize those around you."

5) "Use total candor, which happens to be one of the defining characteristics of effective leaders; there's no need for sugarcoating."

6) "Through it all, never forget that you're a leader now. It's not about you anymore. It's about them."

Brene Brown Writes About Leadership

Brene Brown is a researcher and social worker, who explored feelings of shame, vulnerability, and courage. She determined vulnerability is the core of all feelings, and is a person's strength, not their weakness. Leaders need to embrace vulnerability in order to be courageous. Vulnerability is neither good or bad, as it is a word that represents fear, anxiety and shame, as well as love, joy and passion. Effective leaders embrace, or face head on, both good and bad vulnerabilities. She also explains "Empathy" as the ability to see the world as others see it, and understand another person's feelings. Developing empathy reduces or eliminates insecurity, and builds resilience against adversity. Resilience grows when a person practices hope. That means telling oneself where you want to go and affirming you have the ability to get there. As a leader, you are about setting a vision, and engaging your team with unwavering optimism and expectations to meet that vision. As you set a plan, do you and your team have the courage to take risks and learn from unsuccessful experiences? As you learned earlier, unsuccessful experiences, or setbacks, are learning opportunities and "giving up" represents failure. We

TEAM TIP

Your success as a leader will come not from what you do, but from the reflected glory of your team.

suggest you read Dr. Brown's books *Dare to Lead* and *Daring Greatly*.

Brene Brown, PHD; https://brenebrown.com/

In closing this chapter, changing a company successfully is evolutionary, it's not revolutionary. In revolutions, people die or are needlessly harmed. In evolutions, change becomes a benefit. Accepting change and building flexibility into the organization is a core competency you should strive for. As you begin the process of creating your organization's future, focus on the customer, their needs, and the benefits you can provide for them.

An important feature about working in teams is the ability to develop future leaders. Managers manage processes, budgets, and business assets. Leaders lead people with a vision and with leadership skills. In order to develop good leadership skills, you must continually strive to improve yourself. The next chapter, Personal Development, was designed to help you understand those key issues that impact your ability to change, improve, and enjoy life while working in teams.

CHAPTER 11

PERSONAL DEVELOPMENT

Learning Objective Questions from Chapter 10: The Management Process

✎	*What are the five major components of the EI Process, and what are the key issues for each?*
	1)
	2)
	3)
	4)
	5)
✎	*What are the three strategic positions, and what are their characteristics?*
	1)
	2)
	3)
✎	*What are the three primary thrusts of those positions, and how they relate to the strategic positions?*
	1)
	2)
	3)

PERSONAL DEVELOPMENT

Introduction

This chapter was placed here for a reason. In previous chapters, we covered the process of problem solving, corporate life cycles, and basic management issues. This chapter is about *you*. Who are *you*? Both as an individual and as part of a group? We have learned that nearly half of the people we meet in our assignments care about what they do, but are unhappy with their career or job.

This chapter is about correcting that situation. Even those who have found their career to be in good standing, should read through this for further enhancement. It is about making you a better performer than you are right now. In today's environment, strategy is nothing without passion and vision.

For those who are about to say "oh boy, here come the psychologists!", please take a few minutes to read further. Be mindful that the law of nature states that two moving bodies that come in contact with each other create friction. You are a moving body.

From an anonymous E-mail:

INSTRUCTIONS FOR LIFE

1. Take into account that great love and great achievements involve great risk.

2. When you lose, don't lose the lesson.

3. Follow the three R's: Respect for self, Respect for others, and Responsibility for all your actions.

4. Remember that not getting what you want is sometimes a wonderful stroke of luck.

5. Learn the rules, so you know how to break them properly.

6. Don't let a little dispute injure a great friendship.

7. When you realize you've made a mistake, take immediate steps to correct it.

8. Spend some time alone every day.

9. Open your arms to change, but don't let go of your values.

10. Remember that silence is sometimes the best answer.

11. Live a good, honorable life. Then when you get older and think back, you'll be able to enjoy it a second time.

12. A loving atmosphere in your home is the foundation for your life.

13. In disagreements with loved ones, deal only with the current situation. Don't bring up the past.

14. Share your knowledge. It's a way to achieve immortality.

15. Once a year, go someplace you've never been before.

16. Remember that the best relationship is one in which your love for each other exceeds your need for each other.

17. Judge your success by what you had to give up in order to get it.

Our travels have led us to some interesting people and situations. As teams are formed, change comes about by interaction and sharing. People who are well grounded in basic values tend to rise consistently through life with satisfaction and achievement. They have figured out the lubrication that enables two bodies to make contact with less friction. What are these values? How does your organization move forward with these "values?" Be mindful that Webster's Dictionary defines "values" as "principles, standards, or a quality considered worthwhile or desirable".

Max DePree expressed several leadership values in his book *Leadership is an Art*. "Leaders must take a role in developing, expressing, and defending civility and values." Civility is not about "fashions", but about those concrete pillars that do not change. It is about the dignity of work, the elegance of simplicity, and the responsibility to serve one another. "Leaders are responsible for effectiveness, or doing the right thing." "Leaders are obligated to provide and maintain momentum." Momentum comes from a clear vision of what the organization ought to be, with a well thought out strategy, communicated to all and setting the standard for accountability. "Leaders should leave behind them assets and a legacy." "Assets" are improved financial performance, and a "legacy" is the future leadership of the organization, but fully developed.

James Collins, who co-authored the book *Built to Last*, wrote an article in *Businessweek*, Aug 28, 2000. In his research of 1,435 publicly-held companies, he tried to determine how many of these firms reached "greatness." His term for "greatness" meant that shareholder value (Theory E) grew three times the market average over 15 years.

How many of the companies do you think he found that met the criteria? Only 11. To us that means that it is very tough to improve things consistently, even with all the MBA's and management literature out there.

In another article in the same issue of *Businessweek*, Andrew Grove, cofounder of Intel, was asked about his view of the future and the pace of change taking place. His remarks were insightful. He said, " My left side of the brain is the technology side, and it is very excited. My right side of the brain is a manager's brain. Through 40 years of management, people haven't changed, so I'm a little skeptical." "The business about speed has its limits. Brains don't speed up. The exchange of ideas doesn't really speed up, (but the process of exchange has changed)." "People have a need to work in teams. There is a desire to work with others." In other words, the environment may change rapidly, but people evolve over time.

The volumes of books out there on Theory "O" subjects can fill the town library. Our intention with this chapter is to identify key values that will sustain you as a person as the company changes by this process. There are certain values that cannot change.

We are taking the most popular titles, along with what we believe are the most effective books on the subject. We hope you agree. We will start with Steven Covey's book, *Seven Habits of Highly Effective People.*

The Seven Habits

Covey defined a habit as "the intersection of *Knowledge, skill, & desire*." Creating a habit requires all three working together or it will not sustain itself. Throughout the book, Covey refers to the "production capability" or "PC" of an individual. The PC principle means "to always treat your employees exactly as you want them to treat your best customers." Covey also reviews the paradigms of interdependence, by referring to the Emotional Bank Account.

This account takes both deposits and withdrawals. When you show discourtesy, disrespect, are betraying trust, or threatening, you are making withdrawals from the bank account. When you work to understand another person, to be kind or courteous, to keep a commitment, to clarify expectations, to show personal integrity, such as being loyal, and apologize *sincerely* when you make a withdrawal; those efforts create deposits.

| If you are principle centered..... | | | *Source: "Seven Habits..." Page 124* |
Security	Guidance	Wisdom	Power
• Your security is based on correct principles that do not change regardless of external conditions • You know that true principles can repeatedly be validated in your own life • As a measurement of self improvement, correct principles function with exactness, consistency, beauty, and strength • Your source of security provides you with an immovable, unchanging unfailing core, enabling you to see change as an exciting adventure to make significant contributions.	• You are guided by a compass that enables you to see where you want to go how you will get there • You use accurate data that makes your decisions both implementable and meaningful • You stand apart from life's situations, emotions, and circumstances, and look at the balanced whole. Your decisions and actions reflect both short- and long-term considerations and implications • In every situation, you consciously, and proactively determine the best alternative based on conscience and principles.	• Your judgment encompasses a broad spectrum of long-term consequences & reflects a wise balance & quiet assurance • You see things differently, & thus you think and act differently from the largely reactive world • You see the world in terms of what you can do for the world and its people • You adopt a proactive lifestyle, seeking to serve, and better others • You interpret all of life's experiences in terms of opportunities for learning and contribution.	• Your power is limited only by your understanding and observance of natural law & correct principles & by the natural consequences of the principle themselves • You become self- aware, knowledgeable, proactive person, largely unconfined by the attitudes, behaviors, and actions by others • Your ability to act reaches far beyond your own resources and encourages highly developed levels of interdependency • Your decisions and actions are not driven by financial or circumstantial limitations. You have interdependent freedom • You stand apart from life's situations, emotions, and circumstances, and look at the balanced whole. Your decisions and actions reflect both short- & long- term considerations & implications • In every situation, you consciously, proactively determine the best alternative based on Conscience and Principles.

Source: *Seven Habits of Highly Effective People* by Steven Covey

Habit 1: Be Proactive

Proactivity refers to a person's initiative. Taking initiatives means that you are becoming responsible for your own life. Your behavior is a result of your *decision*, not your *condition*. Covey views responsibility, or "response-ability" as meaning your ability to choose your responses. Reactive people are generally affected by their physical surroundings or social environment. Proactive people are value-driven, producing quality work, regardless of what is going on around them. They focus their efforts on expanding their "circle of influence" in positive ways, rather than negative.

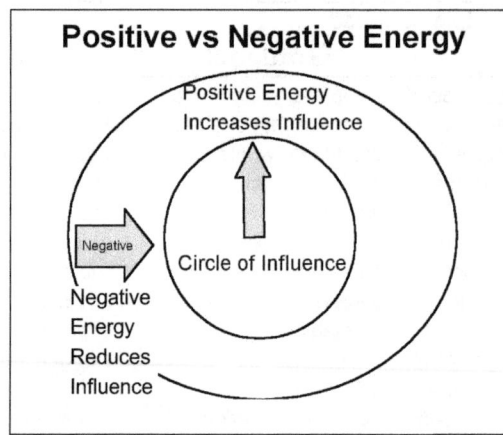

Positive vs Negative Energy

Positive Energy Increases Influence

Circle of Influence

Negative

Negative Energy Reduces Influence

Habit 2: Begin with the End in Mind

Covey suggests you develop a personal mission statement defining what you want to be, much like a company's mission statement. From that mission statement, your principles will begin to form. Covey refers to the term "Principle Centered." If you are principle centered, your four life support factors will align. Those factors are: Security, Guidance, Wisdom, and Power. The chart on the previous page illustrates those elements.

Habit 3: Put First Things First

Covey opened this discussion with two questions:

1. "What one thing could you do (that you aren't doing now) that if you did on a regular basis would make a tremendous positive difference in your personal life?"

2. "What one thing in your business or professional life would bring similar results?"

	Urgent	**Not Urgent**
Important	**Activities:** • Crises • Pressing problems • Deadline driven projects	**Activities** • Relationship building • Planning • Recreation • Prevention • PC Activities
Not Important	**Activities:** • Interruptions • Some calls • Some mail • Some meetings • Pressing matters • Some reports	**Activities:** • Trivia • Busy work • Some mail • Some phone calls • Time wasters • Pleasant activities

Covey refers to the four human endowments of self-awareness, imagination, conscience, and independent will. For this habit, independent will is harnessed by effective self-management. In order to develop good self-management systems, you have to look at the dimensions of: *Important*, *Not Important*, *Urgent*, and *Not Urgent*. The chart above illustrates those four quadrants.

In summary of the chart, the key is to allocate time for Not Urgent and Important, and reduce time in the Not Urgent, Not Important quadrant.

Habit 4: Think Win-Win

There are five dimensions of a Win-Win situation: Character, Relationships, Agreements, Supportive Systems, and Processes.

Character refers to a person's integrity or values, maturity of balancing courage with consideration, and having an "abundance" mentality—meaning there is plenty out there for everyone.

Relationships refers to the trust and emotional bank account balance.

Agreements have five elements:

1. Desired results

2. Guidelines to accomplish the results (policies and, principles)

3. Resources available to enable the results to be achieved

4. Accountability with standards of performance and evaluation

5. Consequences—both good and bad—are clearly defined

Supportive systems are those practices you develop that sustain your efforts in a win-win dimension. Rewards are a common support system.

Processes refers to a person's ability to separate the person from the problem, to attend to a person's interest, not to their positioning approach. It is about creating a way that avoids the pitfalls of a *loss*.

Habit 5: Seek to Understand, then Be Understood

Covey wrote "Seeking to understand requires consideration; seeking to be understood requires courage." It is about good communication: empathic listening, diagnosing the issues before speaking, and being patient with, and respectful of, others.

Habit 6: Synergize

Synergy refers to working jointly for a common end. As Covey put it: "the whole is greater than the sum of its parts." By synergizing, you will create an exciting, catalytic, unifying, and empowering experience for those around you.

It is about creative cooperation. If you differ with someone, affirm with them that you differ, showing respect. "We agree to disagree."

Habit 7: Sharpen the Saw

This habit is about taking care of #1, that being YOU! Covey identifies four dimensions to your well being:

1. **Physical:** refers to exercise, nutrition, and stress management

2. **Mental:** refers to reading, writing, planning, and visualizing

3. **Spiritual:** refers to commitment and value clarification, study and meditation

4. **Social/Emotional:** Service, intrinsic security, synergy, and empathy

Drucker's View

Since knowledge workers are facing extraordinary change, they must ask the following questions:

- *What are my Strengths and Weaknesses?* It is important to develop a personal system of feedback analysis with action conclusions. Key areas to work on include: intellectual arrogance, bad habits, bad manners, and competency.

- *How do I work?* This is about personal performance. Do you acquire knowledge by reading or listening? What systems do you have to develop memory recollection, such as notebooks, calendars, etc.?

- *What are my Values?* Ethics is a value system. Frustration will develop quickly if the organization's values do not mesh with an individual's values.

- *Where do I belong?* Some people thrive as leaders, others as followers. A common term, "the peter principle" relates to a person's natural ascendency into incompetency. Can you lead with others or help get things done by yourself? Knowing where you fit in will enhance your success.

- *Where and how can I make a difference?* Goals that are stretchable and achievable are the best goals. Knowledge workers may ask "Does this contribution fit my strengths?"

- *What do I do with my self when I end my career, but not my life?* With a life expectancy to exceed the normal career, what will you do? Retirement is different for many people. Developing "parallel careers" with volunteer work is one way to make a transition. The key to retirement success is creating the new career *long before* you retire.

- *How do I accept my responsibility to others?* Covey's remarks on responsibility, "the ability to respond," is closely aligned to Drucker's. Several key areas for Drucker include sharing of information, respect, listening, and building trust.

Building Trust

The word "trust" is a very difficult term to describe. The Webster's Dictionary" states: Trust is "a strong belief that a person or thing is honest or can be depended on." As a verb, "to rely on, believe, or depend on."

In a March 1998, *Family Business Review* article, called *The Trust Catalyst in the Family-Owned Business*, Kacie LaChapelle, and Louis Barnes outlined the four characteristics of a "trust catalyst," or a person who builds trust in an organization. These four C's are: Character, Caring, Competency, and Consistency or predictability. The authors wrote:

- "**Character** covers a number of concepts inherent in the basic values of integrity, honesty, and credibility; being perceived as a 'good' person."

- "**Competency** involves skills, expertise, and performance that implies generally sound judgment, and decision-making abilities."

- "**Consistency** or Predictability refers to follow-through, kept promises, and a history of consistent responses and behavior."

- "**Caring** is demonstrated through supportive acts that convey genuine interest in the well-being of others, as well as empathy and understanding."

Of note, we believe that the author's approach is flawed. It focused on success, not on failures. It is our position that people learn more from failures than they do from success. Sports teams modify game plans and players to adjust to the game played, not the season because they know that they are not performing well. Success creates arrogance. Therefore, we contend that by identifying clues to failure, rather than success, teams will continually improve their results and improve consistency. Knowing only that 11 companies fit their criteria doesn't reflect all of the values that companies measure for success.

Dealing with Others

This area of the chapter will refer to the four different roles of management, which were found on the first page of Chapter 8. To refresh your memory, the four roles of management include:

"P"- Producers
"A"- Administrators
"E"- Entrepreneurs
"I"- Integrators

These are suggestions for improving your working relationship with people who exhibit one of the four different roles of management:

When working with "P's":
- If you need help from this person, communicate their indispensability to dealing with this "crisis."

- Get down to business quickly,

- Move rapidly, slowing down when asked to,

- Anticipate action to show initiative,

- Open the conversation with the end result, "Our purpose for this meeting is...".

When working with "A's":

- Do exactly as you said you would,

- Speak slowly, without much emotion,

- Stop along the way to gather objections before they accumulate,

- Do not push for rapid decisions,

- Develop historical perspectives, creating logical outlines of the facts in detail,

- Do not use gimmicks or tricks to prove your point,

- *Always* be prepared to prove your point,
- Prepare your presentation to point out the minimization of risk.

When working with "E's":

- Avoid details unless asked, but be prepared to show them,

- The more visual, exciting, and dramatic the story, the better,

- Allow for input throughout presentation,

- Provide for options, so they own the decision,

- Get decisions down in writing,

- Get consent before showing initiative, it could be viewed as mutiny,

- Be sure to recognize and use their ideas.

When working with "I's":

- Don't push for rapid decisions, unless you have others in support of your recommendation,

- Be prepared to have your support from others verified no matter what the issue,

- To change this person's mind, you should discuss the feelings and opinions of others,

- "Warm up" to that person by showing interest in their personal life; spend time to listen and share.

Individual Accountability

Individual Accountability refers to an objective or task that a person is held responsible for, but who may not perform all of the work. Developing accountability requires communication of objectives, providing proper training and support, and empowering for action. An annual review, such as

definition

Individual Accountability: refers to an objective or task that a person is held responsible for, but who may not perform all of the work.

the accompanying 360 review by GE's Power Systems (Page 142), may help institutionalize the values and competency development needed improve accountability; thus, enabling the employee and business to grow.

Marston's Four Point Model

Dr. William Marston published a book, *The Emotions of Normal People*, in 1928. He described people in four quadrants: Introvert vs. Extrovert, and Task/Thinking vs. Feelings/Relations. The chart below expresses his concepts.

We share this information to you now, so that you can determine how you fit within your team. **Dominant** people create activity in an antagonistic environment. People in the **Influence** area produce activity in a favorable environment. **Steady** people are passive in a favorable environment, and **Compliant** people are passive in an antagonistic environment. We use this model to help others see each other and respect their values in a team. The following paragraphs help to describe the characteristics of each quadrant.

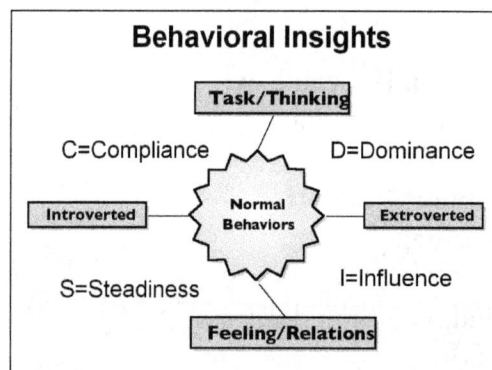

Behavioral Insights

Task/Thinking

C=Compliance   D=Dominance

Introverted   Normal Behaviors   Extroverted

S=Steadiness   I=Influence

Feeling/Relations

Compliant, or how you respond to rules and procedures set by others: You tend to be an accurate, analytical, conscientious, courteous, mature, patient, precise, and diplomatic fact-finder with high standards. Your value to the team involves maintaining high standards, being conscientious and steady, defining, clarifying, getting and testing information, and a person who is an objective and comprehensive problem solver.

Steadiness, or how you respond to the pace of the environment:

> You tend to be an amiable and friendly, a good listener, patient, relaxed, sincere, stable, steady, and an understanding team player. Your value to the team includes being dependable, working for the leader with a cause, being patient and empathic, and a logical and service-oriented step-wise thinker.

Dominance, or how you respond to problems and challenges:

> You can be described as an adventuresome, competitive, daring, decisive, direct, innovative, persistent, results-oriented, self-starting problem solver. Your value to the team includes being a bottom line organizer, being forward looking, challenge-oriented, innovative, and known for initiating activity.

Influence, or how you respond to others to your point of view:

> You are viewed as a confident, charming, convincing, enthusiastic, inspiring, optimistic, popular, sociable, persuasive, and trusting person. Your value to the team includes being a team player, negotiating conflicts, motivating others toward goals, being optimist and enthusiast, and showing a high level of creative problem solving.

It is important that you recognize the values of each team member and the contribution they bring. As you read earlier in the life cycle chapter, it is normal for growing organizations to have conflicts with direction and change, and little with each other. In aging organizations, the inability to adapt or be flexible, while requiring others to get along instead of getting things done, reduces the conflicts on direction, and increases the conflict against each other.

As you go about the team-building process with growth in mind, it is most important that you accept each member

> **TEAM TIP**
>
> *As you go about the team-building process with growth in mind, it is most important that you accept each member of your team as a multi-disciplined or viewed specialist who provides meaningful insights from their point of view!*

of your team as a multi-disciplined or viewed specialist who provides meaningful insights *from their point of view*!

A great way to test this theory is to hold a beach ball between two people who are looking at it from a face-to-face position. As they describe the colors they see, why are they not seeing each other's colors? Why do you, looking from the outside, see the colors? In other words, the ability to see the real picture requires stepping back, and looking at the issues from a distance, rather than from close up. Putting two or more people together requires the acceptance of other points of view, in order to solve problems more effectively.

Creating a Values Statement

There are many forms of values statements. Rather than go through a bunch of words describing the process, review the next page's Value Statement Sample. After you have read it, ask yourself if you understand "Who" they are, and what principles they govern themselves by. What kind of rules do they follow? What is important to them? What isn't?

When you go about developing your values statement, be mindful that they are unshakable, nonnegotiable messages. Keep it simple, and be sure they are the outcomes you desire. A sample Values Statementis on the following page.

Statement of Guiding Values

Norwich University was founded in 1819 by Captain Alden Partridge, U.S. Army, and is the oldest private military college in the country. Norwich University is a diversified academic institution that educates traditional age students in a Corps of Cadets or as civilians, and adult students. Norwich identifies the following as our guiding values.

1. We are men and women of honor and integrity. We shall not tolerate those who lie, cheat, or steal.

2. We are dedicated to learning, emphasizing teamwork, leadership, creativity, and critical thinking.

3. We respect the right to diverse points of view as a cornerstone of our democracy.

4. We encourage service to nation and others before self.

5. We stress being physically fit and drug free.

6. To live the Norwich motto, Essayons!—I will try!—meaning perseverance in the face of adversity.

7. We stress self-discipline, personal responsibility, and respect for law.

8. We hold in highest esteem our people and reputation.

Source: http://www.norwich.edu/about/who/values.html 5/30/2000

E Power Systems: 360 Degree Leadership Assessment Ratings

Source: Corporate Leadership Council, The Next Generation: Accelerating the Development of Rising Leaders P142-143

Leader's Name _____   Coach _____

Rating Scale: Needs Significant Development |--1--2--3--4--5--|

Characteristic	Performance Criteria	Mgr.	Peer	Staff
Vision	• Has developed and communicated a clear simple, customer-focused vision/direction for the organization • Forward thinking, stretches horizons, challenges imagination • Inspires and energizes others to commit to the vision; leads by example • As appropriate, updates the vision, accelerates changes			
Customer/ Quality/Cost	• Listens to customers and assigns the highest priority to customer satisfaction, including internal customers • Inspires a passion for excellence in every aspect of work • Committed to achieving highest product/service quality at competitive market price by streamlining processes/structure • Demonstrates a service mindset and unyielding cost consciousness throughout the organization • Integrates internal and external customer feedback into business • Challenges existing process capability and encourages alternative solutions • Understands the underlying theories and practices of Six Sigma from a management and technical perspective			
Integrity	• Maintains unequivocal commitment to honesty/truth in every facet of behavior • Follows through on commitments; assumes responsibility for own mistakes • Practices absolute conformance with company policies and ethical code • Actions and behaviors are consistent with words. Absolutely trusted by others.			
Communication /Influence	• Communicates in open, candid, clear, complete, and consistent manner inviting response/dissent • Listens effectively and probes for new ideas. Uses facts and rational arguments to influence and persuade • Breaks down barriers and develops influential relationships across teams, functions, and layers			
Accountability/ Commitment	• Sets and meets aggressive commitments to achieve business objectives • Demonstrates courage/self-confidence to stand up for beliefs, ideas, and coworkers • Fair and compassionate, yet willing to make difficult decisions • Demonstrates uncompromising responsibility for preventing harm to the environment			

Leader's Name: Coach:

Rating Scale: Needs Significant Development |— 1— 2 —3 — 4 — 5 —| Outstanding Strength

Characteristic	Performance Criteria	Mgr.	Peer	Staff
Shared Ownership/ Boundary-less	• Self confidence to share information across traditional boundaries and be open to new ideas • Encourages/promotes shared ownership for team vision & goals • Trusts others; encourages risk taking and boundary-less behavior • Champions Work-Out as a vehicle for everyone to be heard. Open to ideas from anywhere			
Team Builder/ Empowerment	• Selects talented people; provides coaching and feedback to develops team members to their fullest potential • Delegates whole tasks; empowers teams to maximize effectiveness. Is personally a team player • Recognizes and rewards progress toward achievement of Six Sigma threshold/objectives • Resources Six Sigma projects and drives Six Sigma culture change. Creates positive work environment			
Diversity	• Demonstrates personal commitment to diversity in staffing, training, development, retention, and related processes. • Uses contemporary change processes to ensure diverse employee participation in continuously improving the business • Actively seeks and considers diverse ideas/approaches in developing alternatives to solve problems/leverage opportunities • Supports employees in balancing work/family demands consistent with personal values and needs of the business			
Knowledge/ Expertise/ Intellect	• Possesses and readily shares functional/technical knowledge and expertise. Constant interest in learning. • Demonstrates broad business knowledge/perspective with cross-functional/multi-cultural awareness • Quickly sorts relevant from the irrelevant information, grasps essentials of complex issues and initiates action • Demonstrates competence and understanding with details of data • Utilizes data to strategically manage the business. Makes good decisions with limited data. Applies intellect to the fullest			
Initiative/Speed	• Anticipates problems and initiates new and better ways of doing things. Creates real and positive change. • Hates/avoids/eliminates bureaucracy and strives for brevity/ simplicity/clarity • Understands and uses speed as a competitive advantage Global Mindset • Demonstrates global awareness/sensitivity and is comfortable building diverse and global teams • Considers the global consequences of every decision. Proactively seeks global knowledge • Treats everyone with dignity and respect.			

CHAPTER 12

ESOPS — BASIC TERMINOLOGY & CONCEPTS

	Learning Objective Questions from Chapter 11: Personal Development
✎	*What is meant by "the Emotional Bank Account?*
✎	*What are the Seven Habits, and what does each mean to you?*
	1)
	2)
	3)
	4)
	5)
	6)
	7)
✎	*What are the Four C's to create TRUST?*
	1)
	2)
	3)
	4)

ESOPS – BASIC TERMINOLOGY & CONCEPTS

This chapter was added later in the book because we learned that in many cases, companies that evolve into ESOPs are not prepared to reap the benefits of being an ESOP. ESOP means "Employee Stock Ownership Plan." Our effort in developing empowered teams reflects the growing needs of ESOP companies to develop their employees to act and perform as owners of the company. This empowerment culture is what we call "the ESOP Ownership Culture." The concept of ESOPs was developed by a set of federal laws under The Employee Retirement Income Security Act of 1974 (ERISA). ERISA is a federal law that sets minimum standards for many pension and health plans in private industry in order to protect individuals, employees or beneficiaries in these plans. Therefore, your ESOP trust is governed just like most retirement plans, such as a 401k, and is regulated by the Federal Government's Department of Labor.

Your ESOP is special because, unlike other companies, your former owners and/or their emerging management team want you to embrace a tested organizational concept of empowering teams to implement change and increase company value. So, what does "empowerment" mean? Empowerment means "the giving or delegation of power; authority." Take the example of a teenage driver. You own three cars: 1) a 10 year old, well maintained Nissan Sentra, 2) a two year old Ford Thunderbird convertible, and 3) a brand new BMW 750Li. By law, your 16 year old child has earned the right to drive, by passing a drivers test, any of these cars. Managing your child's expectations to drive your cars is about your ability to develop your inexperienced driver to drive all three in a graduated way. This takes time, and it requires that the risks be made, and over time the young driver will graduate to the more expensive alternatives. As the young driver matures and gains more experience, the parents' trust rises, allowing the child to drive the more expensive cars.

Using the Example of your Parents' House

Our intention for this chapter is to help, you, the reader

1) understand the basics of an ESOP,

2) learn what we think is its most effective culture, and

3) appreciate the economics that drive the company to exceed expectations.

We think ESOP's are great for employees and their families because an ESOP employee's hard work now puts money in THEIR retirement funds, not just the (former or current) owners. In order to describe the essence of the ESOP concept, we will use the example of your parents owning their home and wanting to retire to southern climates.

Let's assume they have a HUGE house they have owned and cared for over many years. Let's assume you are dealing with your parents' decisions. With all of their children grown up, namely you and your brothers and sisters, who now live out of the house, your parents want to sell their house and move to a smaller house and keep the rest of the money for retirement. All of their retirement capital is in the house value. They don't have much in savings.

Years ago, your parents bought their house, taking a HUGE risk, borrowing a TON of money, in their view, and over many years paid off the mortgage. They worked their butts off to pay off the mortgage and all of your siblings' educational expenses. They also risked investment to grow the house, by buying more land and expanding the rooms. Back then, their house was worth $40,000; today it is now worth $5,000,000. With their choices to sell it to your family or strangers, they chose to sell it to you, their family! For our example, you did not have the money to buy it, so the parents used government tax advantages and bank financing to sell it to you without your money as down payment, and used the house's rental income (or company profit) to pay for the purchase of stock.

As a result, they sold their shares (or deed) to you, through an ESOP trust, so that they lower their taxes on the sale to you, and you own the house without putting down your own money to buy it. In the case of an ESOP company, it is not a house's deed, but shares of a company. The ESOP trust owns company stock and allocates your prorated shares in your name or in the case of our example, they own the deed of the company. Like your parents sharing proportionately the ownership among their children, ESOP shares are allocated to all employees in a proportional way.

The Organization of ESOPS

Some ESOPs are partially owned by family businesses because they wanted to sell a few shares to give a portion of the wealth to their employees, but keep the family in the business. Or, the ESOP was formed to buy out one of several partners or a single owner whose family is not in the company. For some ESOPs, a division of a large company was spun off using an ESOP to save jobs. We usually find former owners of ESOPs to be very caring and progressive CEOs and/or owners who desired to recognize the hard work of their employees by "gifting" the company to them, as parents would do with their children. We commonly use the word "gifting" because the ESOP beneficiary, namely you, did not pay for the stock. The former owner usually takes all the risks of the sale of stock so employees can enjoy a sum for their retirement as a beneficiary; just like the

ESOP Governance Pyramid

Owners set expectations, Directors mentor CEO to meet expectations

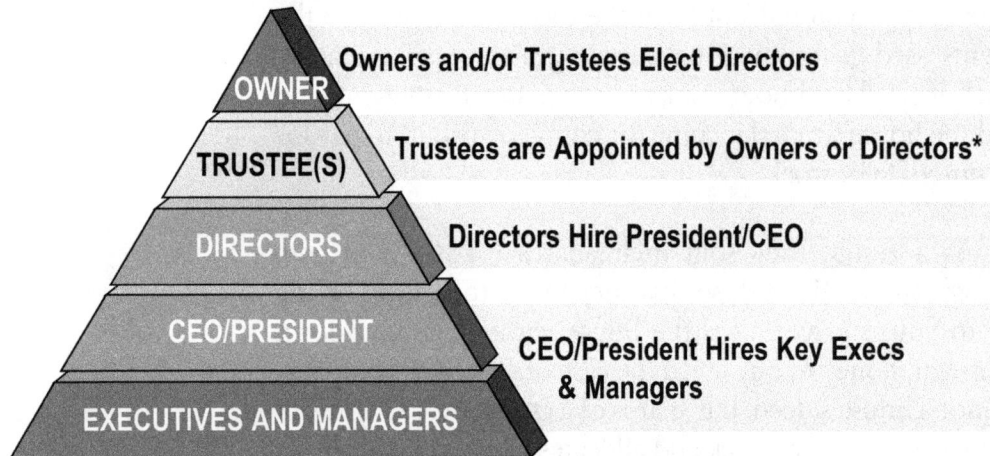

OWNER — **Owners and/or Trustees Elect Directors**

TRUSTEE(S) — **Trustees are Appointed by Owners or Directors***

DIRECTORS — **Directors Hire President/CEO**

CEO/PRESIDENT

EXECUTIVES AND MANAGERS — **CEO/President Hires Key Execs & Managers**

*For mature ESOPs, the ESOP Committee can appoint the Trustees

former owners had, but without the employee putting any money in the company or taking any risk. A beneficiary is a person who receives and enjoys the rights to money or asset value. ESOP beneficiaries have legal protections to ensure their benefits are real and protected. There are owners who sell their shares to the trust for a very attractive tax benefit, while others desire to share the wealth with their employees. They chose not to sell their shares to an outside firm, who could have paid a large "strategic premium," and could have terminated employees to cover that "premium." In many cases, these owners chose not to give or sell their shares to their own family directly. And with ESOPs over time, they continue the legacy for future generations of people.

It is important to know an ESOP trust requires a "Trustee" to be selected. A Trustee is a person, employee group, or outside financial institution responsible for making sure the Trust is properly managed, a Trustee should want increased stock value through their company's growth and prosperity. The Trustee, as a fiduciary, is personally liable for not following ERISA Rules. In most cases, the Trustee's responsibility is to vote for Directors of the Board. The pyramid to the left represents the power of the company, and at the top of the pyramid are the owners, then the trustees.

Another aspect of ESOPS you need to know: does your ESOP trust own LESS than 50% of the outstanding stock shares or does the trust own MORE than 50% of the outstanding shares? If the trust owns less than 50% of the outstanding shares, the control of the company rests on someone other than the ESOP Trustee. This means the board of directors could be selected by the majority shareholders who are not ESOP trustees. In other words, the direction of the company could rest on the investors or founding owners (or CEO), and/or possibly their family.

> **definition**
>
> *Trustee:*
> is a person, employee group, or outside financial institution responsible for making sure the Trust is properly managed, and the ESOP share value grows and management grows

In many cases it is permitted for the founders (former business owners), or in the case of your house, Mom and Dad, to be the Trustees, and control the votes for as long as they wish. This sometimes makes sense because they are risking the value of their house NOW, with the intent that you benefit from the future value. They will sign personal guarantees to ensure the bank will fund the buyout. They may also invite one or all of their key managers to be trustees, so they get used to caring for the company. We have found that future generations must take risks to buy out their preceding generations; otherwise they don't appreciate owning the company.

With an ESOP, there are governing structures you should be aware of. Employees are beneficiaries, and have trustees and ESOP committees who will help you understand the value of being an ESOP, and will speak to management to ensure the company is going in the right direction. The management team is governed by advisory and governing boards, with members on those boards elected or appointed by the Trustee.

ESOP Governance Structures

FAMILY COUNCIL		ADVISORY BOARD

Family

Family Managers with Stock

Management

Cousins   Founder

Family Employees

CEO?

Non-Family Partners

Next Gen   Key Mgrs

Employees

Key Employee

Owners/Trustees

ESOP COMMITTEE		GOVERNING BOARD

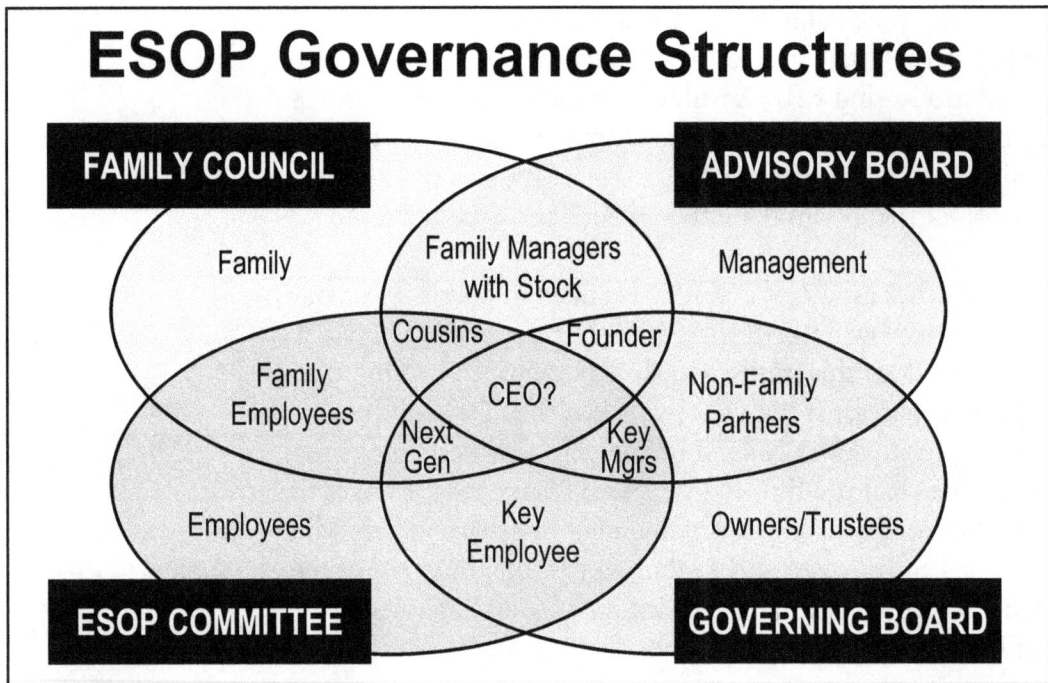

The above chart shows the interlocking relationships of a typical ESOP. The four circles (Family, Employee, Management and Ownership) represent the various roles of each position of authority.

Some things to consider at times:

1) The above chart shows the CEO is in a complex situation because he or she may be wearing many hats and roles, and may NOT be the former owner but a long term and trusted key manager whom the former owner or board elected to be the next CEO

2) Advisory Boards advise management on best practices and strategy and mentor new CEO's in a leadership change; Governing boards, who are comprised of successful executives, have authority to hire and fire the CEO and management team

3) the Trustee has the power to elect or un-elect directors and advisors, select the price of the stock, and ensure stock transactions are fair to the employees.

4) The ESOP Committee is responsible for improving the organization's ownership culture through communication programs and events. They may also have the responsibilities of administering the ESOP compliance reports and forecasting employee retirements.

We do not want to minimize the importance of the ESOP Committee, because in mature ESOP's the ESOP Committee can play an important role as the authority to appoint the trustee. The Board usually selects beneficiaries of the ESOP trust to be on the ESOP Committee to help develop the ESOP interest, set the stock expectations, and work with management to build stock value for everyone's benefit.

TEAM TIP

Every Employee-owner should receive and carefully read their SPD.

The purpose of the ESOP trust is to allow the company to continue while sharing the wealth of the Company's stock value among the beneficiaries, namely you! In the case of an ESOP, a beneficiary is any person on the payroll who receives a W2 set for a minimum number of hours during the fiscal year, or their named beneficiaries in case of death. To learn more, you should have received a "Summary Plan Description" or SPD which is a legal document that outlines how the ESOP Trust will work, how beneficiaries earn stock, and how the company's Trustee will manage the trust on behalf of YOU. In some cases, the ESOP Trust has "Pass-Through Voting" features for certain events. For example, if the company was negotiating the sale of the company to another company or investor, a "Pass-Through Voting" feature would give all the employees the right to vote for or against the sale of the company.

Financial Matters

A common ESOP term is "Repurchase Obligations." Repurchase obligations represents the amount of money needed to repurchase the outstanding shares from the ESOP trust to transfer that money to the retiring beneficiary. Since the company is legally responsible or required to buy back the retiree's shares, they have choices in how they buy shares. The company has two basic options for purchasing a retiree's shares; 1) sell them to the trust and trustee who will "recycle" these shares under the same formula as described in the SPD; or 2) reduce the number of shares outstanding, thus the remaining shareholders increase their percentage of ownership. Of great concern is the company's ability to fund repurchase obligations, as people retire and want their money out. In addition, beneficiaries over 55 years old and have at least 10 years of service in the plan have the option of selling their shares to buy other publicly held company shares to diversify their portfolio of stock. Managing and forecasting repurchase obligations requires serious financial planning. If not managed well, the reduction of cash or the increase of debt will drop the stock price and will impact the company's ability to grow. Therefore, it is very important that the trustee as well as management be aware of these fiduciary issues.

Another thing you should be aware of is how the company files its tax returns. For Income Tax purposes, the company is a corporation, not a partnership, so it is either a "C Corporation" or an "S Corporation." An "S" corporation reports revenues and expenses the same way as a "C" corporation, with one very important benefit as this book is being written: The company's net profit becomes the Income for the ESOP Trust, a tax free entity. Therefore, profits from "S" corporations are not taxed, and the money remains in the company. With "C" corporations, the Net profit IS taxed, therefore the company has less money staying in the company for future needs. Once a company is more than 50% ESOP owned, it is usually very beneficial to become an "S" corporation. That allows the untaxed money to stay in the company and fund repurchase obligations for those who will be retiring in the next few years. It also allows the company to have cash to reinvest in new machinery, equipment or to help fund expanding products or locations.

What we want YOU to know is that for the company to grow, it needs to take risks. It may need to borrow money to acquire another company. It may need to hire more people to expand its marketplace and market share. It may need to risk profits at the cost of today's stock value to fund new products and services, in order to meet customer demands. All of these decisions are about improving future profits for the company; however, they may result in smaller employee pay raises. This commonly creates conflict because employees want pay raises, and the board and Trustee want increased stock prices for your retirement. This conflict is normal, as it reflects business decisions, and business is about risk. If you ask the founders if they took pay cuts to help the company, they will ALL tell you they did. Their focus was not on their current pay, but for value when it was time to sell. With an ESOP, management tries to balance these conflicting interests so the younger people have something for their retirement.

How You Can Grow Your ESOP

Your role as a beneficiary is to actively involve yourself with teams and team development. By volunteering to join a team, you will learn more about the company through problem-solving efforts and workflow changes. This way, your efforts will impact the value of the stock and the company's performance, as well as your own personal development and value to the company. With increased profits, there is more money to share in pay raises and bonuses as well. An ESOP with flat sales over many years, or lack of investment in new products or services, will immediately impact your company's ability to pay bills and pay you a raise. If you embrace

> **TEAM TIP**
>
> *By actively involving yourself with teams and team development, you will help the company grow, and thereby increase the value of the shares, which can lead to pay raises and bonuses*

the concepts of team leadership, and apply problem solving techniques using teams, you and your fellow beneficiaries will enjoy the stock's price rise in value, and increase the chances for pay raises. And to repeat what has been already said, it is very important for team empowerment to be evolutionary, not revolutionary. Learning how to drive a car takes time to build trust, as it does for teams and leaders to evolve and build trust with management.

We desire you, the reader, to become a loyal shareholder, with your trustee, in order to increase the stock value over many years, which will keep your job safe and secure. Year by year, your stock price will fluctuate, or change up and down, just like the publicly held companies. Properly managed ESOP companies create value to all shareholders, and attract new employees, who can help the company grow further. We have met several "millionaires;" those retired ESOP employees who were paid over $1 million at their retirement. They will tell you they made more money from the ESOP than they did on their 401k. This is why we want YOU to understand how ESOPs can be great for you and your family.

So you now work for an ESOP owned company, and are now an ESOP beneficiary, or you have been one for some time. What are the next levels of the ESOP's evolution? We have studied many ESOPs, and have determined that the best approach towards an ownership culture depends on empowering teams, and to develop leaders, not managers, to take risks, create change, and identify growth opportunities. With teams you have the opportunity to impact and improve your stock value and job security. In our travels, we have found managers who will not embrace empowered teams, as they have witnessed or heard about poor execution and follow through from teams. Or they fear they will lose control over you and your performance. At this point in the book, you have learned that empowerment and leadership are intertwined and necessary to drive up sales and profits for future pay raises. We believe having sponsors accountable for a team's success changes the dynamics and produces effective results.

There are several associations that promote and support ESOP education, including The ESOP Association (www. esopassociation.org), and the National Center of Employee Ownership (NCEO) (www.nceo.org). We include this here so you can look them up on the internet. We also want you to know that the typical ESOP conflicts usually resolve themselves over time as the annual shareholder letters indicate improvement and the company's leadership begins to embrace the new social order. ESOPs inherently are so complex that everyone must be educated on how ESOPs work before they can allow others to embrace the change. By having you read this book, it indicates your management team's commitment to having the ESOP "ownership" culture work for YOU, not someone else. By teaching teamwork, leadership development, and open book management, you now begin the process of empowering everyone to contribute and benefit each other. You are now more educated to improve your company's stock value and create security for yourself and other employees. Hopefully by now, you are experiencing the value of working in a team to impact the company.

CHAPTER 13

GETTING
RESULTS

	Learning Objective Questions from Chapter 12: ESOPs
✏	*What is meant by "the Emotional Bank Account?*
✏	*What are the Seven Habits, and what does each mean to you?*
	1)
	2)
	3)
	4)
	5)
	6)
	7)
✏	*What are the Four C's to create TRUST?*
	1)
	2)
	3)
	4)

GETTING RESULTS

Introduction

For the final chapter, we are combining the eleven previous chapters into action. Over the next few months you will be learning new ways to improve processes and methodologies. The goal is to empower you and your teams with improved action and performance. The real test is for your organization to achieve 'hands-on' problem-solving abilities and success.

Our experience has shown that once the teams begin functioning, the need for further team facilitation will diminish. Our goal in a team-building process is to "set it up, allow for a transition, and get out of the way" as soon as possible. Your goal should be to reposition yourselves and the company for future growth.

What's Next?

Gerry Faust, Dick Lyles, and Will Phillips wrote in *Responsible Managers get Results* that there are two ways to create profits: Constructive and Destructive.

Constructive Profits are the resulting long-term values created for the intention of owners, customers, and employees. **Destructive Profits** are driven by the short-term efforts of cost cutting for the sake of improving profitability.

During most of the last twenty five years of the 1900s, change in business came about by hiring consultants to cut costs, and improve cycle times and efficiencies. Corporate raiders like Carl Icahn were known to create change and stockholder value by force. Their ability to buy large stakes in the victim's stock, change the board and CEO, and begin dismantling businesses, or ruthlessly chopping off expenses created "shareholder value." That is not what this process is about.

Our approach through this CSI workbook is to teach you a different way of improving your company's profitability through constructive change. Losing sight of what the business is about and how change improves things is the most common cause of failure during changes.

Other factors that cause change to fail include the lack of leadership support and continual communication, not recognizing the difference between change (the desire for something new) and a transition process (the road map to go from 'A' to 'Z'), avoidance of pain or failure, and by not balancing doing the job with doing the job better.

First Year Implementation

Please review page 10 to refresh your memory of how first year implementation works. From Covey's Circle of Influence, in which you can only change what is inside the circle, not outside it, we know that it is the same for implementation. The team approach addresses the size of each person's small circle of influence and increases it. Here are some thoughts about improving the odds of implementation:

- Changes rarely flow up river, so make sure changes are implemented at or near the top first.

- Identify the "Champion" or "Change Agent" who will own the change process.

- Leadership must show by example, and be accountable for results.

- Implement those changes to improve strengths first, rather than weaknesses. This way, the chances of success rise.

- Maintain a pace that minimizes resistance to change, increasing the pace over time. Turning a "donkey" into a "race horse" will take time.

Developing Goals

Webster's Dictionary defines the word "goal" as follows:

"The purpose toward which an endeavor is directed; an end; an objective."

Drucker's view of goals (or objectives) consists of this statement: "Objectives are needed in every area where performance and results directly and vitally affect the survival and prosperity of the business." In other words, organizations cannot have just one goal, they must develop many. Management is about prioritizing and balancing these goals, as well as defining them. A key performance or management competency indicator is a manager's ability to arrive at goals that harmonize the different needs of the business, rather than the skills that make the goals. It is effectiveness versus efficiency.

Covey views goal-setting as a process (from Habit #2 on page 132, "Beginning with the End in Mind"). Things are created twice, once by the idea, and the second by the result. Without the idea or goal, there are very few results. It is important to note that it is the second habit out of seven, meaning that it comes before everything else, other than the habit of "Being Proactive." Getting results requires you to be proactive and setting goals.

Properly developed goals are used as "landmarks," guiding the management team as to where they are, where they came from, and how far they are from "getting there." A bus driver relies on maps, signs, and the driver's display panel to know what is going on and where he/she is. Bad goals are better than no goals, at least the driver knows which direction to take, whether it's right or wrong. Highly developed organizations develop goals so that bus drivers meet their customer needs, are on time and at the right locations. In return, the customer expects performance and values it.

TEAM TIP

Properly developed goals are used as "landmarks," guiding the management team as to where they are, where they came from, and how far they are from "getting there."

213

Goals are not mission and vision statements. Mission and vision statements are the framework of "purpose and direction," creating mental models of an organization. These statements, as described on page 156, help an organization work together rather than separately or independently. The power of a vision and mission statement shows up when the organization faces a remarkable change, or threat, forcing senior management to allow lower levels to contribute to key decisions in order to survive. Goals are measurements of achievement, not the purpose or direction of an organization. For example, if your personal vision and mission statement is to be healthy and active after you retire, your goals may include exercising (lose 15 pounds) and developing new skills (join a non-profit board or learn golf) that will provide enjoyment and interaction.

There are nine basic tests that make up a good goal:

1. Does the goal help organize and guide many activities into a simple form?
2. Is the goal easily understood and measurable to allow management to test the value within the time span.
3. Is the time span reasonable?
4. Does the goal meet the values and expectations of the leadership?
5. Will the goal motivate for action?
6. Is the goal visible and tangible?
7. Does the goal predict behavior?
8. Does the goal help management analyze their activities and experience?
9. Does the goal provide a measurement to appraise management's decisions?

SMART Goals are a coined term for the above 9 tests. The letters S.M.A.R.T. represent the following: S=Specific, M=Measurable, A=Achievable, R=Relevant (or Tangible),

definition

SMART Goals
S = Specific
M = Measurable
A = Achievable
R = Relevant
T = Time-Bound

and T=Time Based. Whether you subscribe to our 9 tests or the more simplistic SMART tests, both help clarify and test goals for their effectiveness.

Long-Range Goals (LRG) are actually milestones in a journey of growth, measuring outcomes over 15 years or so, as opposed to a **Short Term's** (STG) 3-5 years. As such, LRG's are visionary, and revised infrequently with little detail. STG's are revised annually, and are typically budgets or forecasts; thus, they're stretchable and reachable. In some cases, goals are "Big & Hairy," or "BAHGs" to help the organization develop aggressive action plans and high expectations.

For example, if a long-term goal is to improve profitability to reduce debt to zero in five years, then a short-term goal is to increase net profit from 1% of sales to something greater that 1% this year. Budgets should reflect change to meet that net profit improvement. Certain product mixes should be identified to improve gross margins, and expenses should be adjusted to make this year's budget goal. Each department will provide both their long-term and short-term goals that commit to the overall plan.

To paraphrase Will Rogers, "Be careful of what you wish for, because chances are you will get what you wish!" Covey describes poor goal-setting as climbing a ladder, only to find that the ladder was on the wrong wall. Poor long-range goals lack sound judgment, intuitive insight, access to voluminous information (not data), and broad knowledge/experience. A teenager's view of a long-range goal on the stock market would be very different from a floor specialist on the New York Stock Exchange. Who would YOU rely on to handle your retirement money?

It should be clear by now that making effective goals and building effective communication up and down the organization requires teams. As a result, teams can provide a diversified view of experiences, knowledge, and an exchange of ideas, as well as voluminous information—to avoid "placing the ladder on the wrong wall."

215

Rewards

Rewarding and Recognizing (R&R) good performance has a tremendous amount of risk to it. Why? When R&R's do not meet the recipient's expectations, anger or confusion develops. When R&R's exceed expectations, they create further prospects for future R&R's, setting a precedent that will be expected to be repeated over and over again. If you automatically give 3% raises every year, regardless of performance, then how will the employees feel when you shift that number up or down?

R&R's come in all sorts of ways. There are *Monetary R&R's* that are given as bonuses, stock options, and pay raises. *Benefit R&R's* are items that are expensed by the company, but are not taxable to the employee all the time. They include: First Class Travel, Club Memberships, Automobile and other Reimbursements. *Acknowledgment R&R's* consist of events and gifts that reward a person without much expense. These R&R's come in the form of certificates, days off, verbal and written acknowledgments, and special events that recognize good performance.

There are hundreds of books out there about this subject, such as *1001 ways to Reward Employees*, by Bob Nelson and Ken Blanchard. However, the key to rewarding is to do it in a timely manner, and rewarding for *improved* performance. It is the ultimate signal from the leadership that a person meets or exceeds expectations. It should be done carefully and with a frequency that does not lessen the appeal or importance.

Key Result Area (KRA's)

We learned about measurements, KPI's, and Balanced Scorecards in Chapter 6. It is now the time to balance these measurements with compensation plans. In developing strategic systems, rewarding and recognizing people is the final action to be developed. The chart on page 153 represents an illustration of the relationships and how performance and rewards should be weighted.

However, as we conclude this CSI workbook with KRA's, it is important for you to understand that this is the beginning of a journey, rather than the end or the middle. This journey requires your commitment to embracing change and continual improvement. KRA's will change as you and the organization change. Since there are no guarantees in life other than death and taxes, KRA's are not permanent nor inflexible.

In many assignments, we begin the process of developing KRA's by the use of a 360 degree, "Balanced Scorecard (BSC) Assessment tool called: Capability Snapshot™. Our purpose for using this tool is to identify your organization's major strengths and weaknesses, opportunities, and threats (SWOT) by the four major BSC components as described in Chapter 6. From that assessment, we will guide your team efforts to improve performance.

As a 360 degree assessment, our survey will view the perspectives of managers, employees, customers, and stakeholders. The value for this form of measuring tool is to provide an outside perspective to your planning process. By having the internal point of view on strategic issues, you can then develop those competencies that will lead to increased market share, improved profitability, and enhanced customer retention. The assessment will collect information by the following BSC strategic challenges:

Operational Effectiveness: issues relating to the way things are done, such as cost management, time utilization, and quality improvement.

Organizational Agility: issues relating to the organization's ability to adapt to change, such as rethinking strategy, redesigning structure, and reengineering processes.

Customer Satisfaction: issues that relate to delivering outstanding value to customers, such as customer focus, customer value, and customer partnering.

Innovation Opportunities: Areas that relate to the realization of breakthrough innovations, such as product/service development, market foresight, and knowledge leveraging.

Learning Culture: the conditions that support continuous learning, such as Employee involvement, Competence Development, and Teamwork commitment.

You are now prepared to create new innovative ways to improve customer and employee satisfaction, operational performance, and the survivability of the organization. The next few months will require more time commitment on your part, since the effort to implement problem-solving processes will consume more time than most figure or expect.

At this juncture, you should now be on a functional team, building process maps, or improving them. The next step is to develop cross functional teams to begin either the action plans from a management retreat or developing costing models to identify value stream mapping opportunities. We hope you will volunteer to be a leader of a team. If you do, you will be sending a message to your company's managers that you want to grow and as a result your opportunities to advance will rise as the company grows.

As you think back through this experience, we would like to hear from you. Let us know what you think about our CSI workbook. Share with us your ideas on how to improve the CSI workbook. If you are so moved, kind words are always appreciated, as well as unkind words. You can contact us any way you want using the information below:

Mail to: Jack Veale
PTCFO, Inc.
48 Walkley Rd
West Hartford, CT 06119
Fax: (860) 232-9438
Phone: (860) 232-9858
Email: jackv@ptcfo.com

GOOD LUCK!

Group	KRA's	Measurements	Weight
Top Team			
Current Performance	Current Financial	Stock Value Added EPS Growth ROI	33% 33% 33% **100%**
Strategic Perform'ce	Strategic Numbers Service Quality Innovation People	 Index Index % new Prods in Mkt Succession Plan Satisfaction Index Cust.Value Index	30%
	Market Position Priority Issue Teams Departmental Plans	Market Share% Objective Met% Strategic Objective% Delegated Departmental Infrastructure	20% 20% 20%
	Team Operations		10% **100%**
Departments			
(On-going Tasks)	Numbers / Metrics Operating Priorities	Sales Gross Margin Budget Performance Service Index Market Penetration New Prod Launch New Prod Slated for next year	25% 5% 10% 20% 20% 20% **100%**

Notes:

_____

_____

_____

_____

_____

_____

_____

_____

Index

Symbols
360 review 188

A
Acknowledgment R&R's 216
Action Plan 7, 26, 45, 49, 63, 73, 74
Adaptive Processes 160, 161
Adizes, Ichak 35, 123
Advisory Boards 202
Agenda 24, 25, 26, 27
Aging Organization 133, 189
Agreements 128, 181, 182
Andrew Grove 178
Aristocracy 132
Arrogance 112, 128, 130, 183
Assets 99, 101, 102, 104, 105, 106, 115, 138, 171, 177
Auerbach, Red 93

B
BAHG 215
Balanced Scorecard (BSC) 21, 98, 99, 115, 216
Ballot Box approach 56
Barrier to entry 152
Beach ball 190
Beneficiary 199, 200, 203, 204, 205, 206
Benefit R&R's 216
Benefit segmentation 118
Best Product 159
Blanchard, Ken 115, 216
Bowles, Sheldon 115
Brainstorming 49, 51, 56, 57, 63, 68, 88
Brown, Brene 171, 172

C
Cause & Effect 49
Cause & Effect Diagrams 49
Change Agents 16, 114
Change Leaders 146
COGS 103, 104
Command 36, 38
Competing for the Future 56, 139, 162
Compliant 188
Consensus 36, 39, 49, 157
Constructive Profits 211
Consultant 113, 123, 137, 211
Consultive style 39
Cookies 82, 87, 161

Core Competencies 118, 156, 157, 162, 164
Core Competency 97, 162, 164, 171
Corporate Life Cycles 123, 175
Cost of Good Sold 103
Courtship 125, 126, 128
Covey 178, 180, 181, 182, 183, 184, 212, 213, 215
Credit 87, 101, 129
Cross Functional Teams 20, 26, 218
Culture 9, 34, 113, 151, 153, 169, 193, 218
Current Ratio 105
Customer Focus 81, 217
Customer Requirements 8, 67, 81
Customer Solutions 160
Cycle Time 17, 18, 19, 58, 95, 96
Cycle Times 65, 68, 98, 100, 137, 211

D
Data 47, 49, 50, 51, 52, 53, 54, 55, 73, 85, 86, 87, 88, 94, 97, 98, 106, 116, 117, 157, 193, 215
Debit 101, 104
Debt to Equity 106
Decision Analysis 144
Delegation 36, 37, 38, 127, 128, 154, 157
Deming 17, 24, 67, 81, 137, 138
Depreciation 102, 105
Destructive Profits 211
Differentiation 159
Directional Statements 156
Dominance 125, 189
Drucker 33, 81, 137, 138, 139, 141, 143, 144, 145, 146, 183, 184, 213

E
EBITDA 105
Economic Models 115, 116
EI process 151, 155
Eleven Laws of Systems Thinking 46
Empowerment 168, 193, 197, 206
Entrepreneur 36, 120, 125
Entropy 111
ERISA 197, 201
ESOP 197, 198, 199, 200, 201, 202, 203, 204, 205, 206, 207
ESOP Committee 201, 203
ESOP Governance Pyramid 200
ESOP Governance Structures 202
ESOP Ownership Culture 197
ESOP Trust 197, 199, 200, 201, 203, 204
Experimentation 125, 161
Experts 24, 77
External Factors 151, 152
Extrovert 188

F

Faust, Gerry 45, 151, 211
Feedback 16, 35, 81, 85, 88, 92, 94, 95, 113, 114, 126, 161, 170, 183, 192, 193, 223, 224
Feelings/Relations 188
Fiduciary 201, 204
Flowchart 68, 70
Flow charting 70
Forming 9, 22, 45
FORMING 22
Founder's trap 128
Functional Teams 19, 20, 218
Fundamental Laws of Thermodynamics 45

G

GAAP 102
Gantt 49, 64
GANTT 63, 65
Generally Accepted Accounting Practices 102
GE's Power Systems 188
Gifting 199
Goals 73, 97, 99, 100, 101, 112, 113, 115, 119, 138, 153, 164, 168, 184, 189, 193, 213, 214, 215
Go-Go 127, 129
Goldratt, Eli 19, 22, 93
Gouillart 114, 115, 116, 118, 120
Gouillart, Francis 114
Governing Boards 201, 202
Gross Profit 103, 104
GUNG HO 115

H

Hall, Doug 57
Hamel, Gary 56, 139, 162
Hammer and Champy 160
Hax, Arnoldo 159
High Performance Team 9, 16, 73

I

IBM 112
Individual Accountability 187
Individual Learning 119
Infant 127
Influence 115, 165, 180, 188, 189, 192, 212
Information 5, 6, 9, 17, 18, 21, 26, 28, 29, 33, 37, 38, 39, 40, 52, 57, 75, 81, 82, 85, 86, 87, 94, 95, 97, 98, 118, 144, 160, 162, 167, 184, 188, 193, 215, 217, 218
Innovation 5, 9, 17, 22, 99, 114, 120, 125, 126, 139
Integration 35, 36, 125, 138
Internal Coaches 21
Introvert 188
Intuition 166, 167
Inventory Turns 105
ISO 9000 5, 67

J

Job rotation 144

K

Kaizen 7
Kelly, James 114
Key Result Area 216
Knowledge workers 145, 183, 184
KRA 216, 217, 219

L

Landry, Tom 94
Law of Thermodynamics 111
LCL 53, 55
Leaders 114, 144, 146, 165, 166, 167, 168, 169, 171, 177, 184
Leadership Team 16, 20, 118
Lean principles 58
Lean Six Sigma 58
Learning Organization 46
Liability 101, 124
Life Cycle 8, 123, 124, 125, 128, 175, 189
Liquidity Ratios 105
Lone Rangers 34, 40
Long-Range Goals 215
Lower Control Limit (LCL) 53, 55
Lyles, Dick 45, 211

M

Management by Objectives 138
Marketing Plan 140, 141
Marston, William 188
Matrix structure 119
MBO 138
Mission Statement 180, 214
Mobilization 114
Monetary R&R's 216
Multifunctional Team 19, 20

N

Normal problems 123
Norming 63, 87, 88

O

Objectives 138, 153, 162, 187, 192, 193, 213
Operating Profit 104
Operating Ratios 106
Owner's Equity 104, 106
Owners' Equity 102

P

Pareto 49, 52, 53, 82
Pass-Through Voting 203
Pathological problems 123
Performing 34, 63, 87, 116, 124, 128, 185
Pert 49
PERT 64, 65, 70
Pinpointing 49, 50, 73
Prahalad, CK 56, 162
Premature Empowerment 35
Prime 129, 130
Problem Solving 8, 28, 45, 47, 49, 51, 53, 55, 57, 59, 62, 65, 67, 69, 71, 73, 75, 77, 80, 158
Problem Statement 50, 73
Procedure 65, 66, 67, 68, 70
Process Improvement 67
Process Map 65, 70, 73, 111, 218
Producer 35, 36, 124, 128, 129, 185
Profit after Taxes 104
Purpose of a Business 81, 139

Q

Quality 7, 17, 18, 81, 84, 96, 155, 192, 219

R

Receivable Days 105
Reframing 114
Relational Map 72
Relational Mapping 71
Renewal 114, 119
Renewing 114
Repurchase Obligations 204, 205
Responsible Managers get Results 45, 211
Restructuring 114, 115
Return on Assets 106
Return on Equity 99, 106
Revitalizing 114
Rewards 22, 100, 119, 131, 154, 158, 182, 216
Rewards and Recognition 22, 154, 158
Reward Systems 113, 119
Robotics 65, 68, 117
Round Robin approach 56
Run Charts 49, 53, 95

S

Scorecards 10, 16, 22, 93, 94, 95, 97, 98, 100
Score Keeping 21
Senge, Peter 46, 117
Short-Term Goals 215
Six Sigma 55, 193
Sloan Management Review 159
Small Business Unit (SBU) 119

SMART Goals 214
Spontaneous Approach 56
Stable 9, 130, 189
Standard Deviation 53, 54, 55
Statistical Process Control 7, 137
Statistical Process Control (SPC) 7
Steadiness 189
Storming 87
Strategic Plan 5, 111, 151, 156, 157
Strategic planning 156
Strategic Planning 164
Strategic Positioning 159
Summary Plan Description (SPD) 203
Survey 85, 86, 87, 88, 96, 97, 98, 141, 217
System Lock-In 160, 163

T
Task/Thinking 188
Taylor, Frederick W. 137
Team Leader 23, 25, 74
Team Member 17, 20, 23, 24, 26, 28, 33, 34, 35, 70, 73, 189, 193
The Delta Model 159
The Fifth Discipline 46, 117
The Goal 93, 116
Theory E 112, 138, 177
Theory O 112, 113, 138
The Practice of Management 33, 137, 138
Thomke, Stefan 161
Total Quality Management (TQM) 7
Trust 19, 33, 34, 36, 38, 120, 141, 179, 181, 184, 197, 198, 199, 200, 201, 203, 204, 206
Trustee 200, 201, 203, 205

U
Upper Control Limit (UCL) 53, 55

V
Value Chain 115, 163, 166
Value Delivery System 118, 119
Value Propositions 118, 119
value stream mapping 58, 218
Values 16, 115, 145, 156, 183, 190, 191
Vision Statement 157, 214

W
Welch, Jack 112, 113, 170
Wilde, Dean 159
Will Phillips 45, 151, 211
Win-Win 181, 182
Working Capital 104
Written Questionnaires 86

Sources

The Balanced Scorecard, Robert Kaplan & David Norton, Harvard Business School Press, 1996
ISBN: 0-87584-651-3

Businessweek, *Visionary vs Visionary*, John Byrne, James Collins, August 28, 2000, P. 212-214; "Don't Rewrite the Rules of the Road," August 28, 2000 P. 206-208, "Ideas The Welch Way" Jack & Suzy Welch, January 30, 2006

Corporate Life Cycles, Ichak Adizes, Prentice Hall, 1988
ISBN: 0-13-174426-7

Competing For the Future, Gary Hamel, C.K. Prahalad, Harvard Business School Press, 1994
ISBN: 0-87584-716-1

The Deming Management Method, Mary Walton, Perigee Publishing, 1986
ISBN: 0-399-55000-3

Family Business Review, *The Trust Catalyst in the Family Owned Business*, Kacie LaChapelle & Louis Barnes, March 1998 Vol XI No. 1

The Fifth Discipline, Perter M. Senge, Currency Doubleday, 1990
ISBN: 0-385-26095-4

The Goal, Eliyahu M. Goldratt & Jeff Cox, North River Press, 1986
ISBN 0-88427-061-0

Gung Ho!, Ken Blanchard & Sheldon Bowles, William Morrow & Co. 1998
ISBN: 0-688-15428-X

Harvard Business Review, *Cracking the Code of Change*, Michael Beer & Nitin Nohria, May-June 2000 Volume 78 No. 4; *Enlightened Experimentation: The New I*

Imperative for Innovation, Stefan Thomke, Feb 2001 Vol 75 No. 2.

Inc. Magazine, *Jump Start Your Business*, John Grossman, May 1997 P. 36-54

Leadership is an Art, Max DePree, Dell Publishing, 1989
ISBN: 0-440-50324-8

Loving Monday, John D. Beckett, Intervarsity Press, 1998
ISBN: 0-8308-1926-6

Management Challenges for the 21st Century, Peter F. Drucker, Harper Business, 1999
ISBN: 0-88730-998-4

The Practice of Management, Peter F. Drucker, Harper & Row, 1954
ISBN: 0-88730-613-6

Predatory Marketing, C. Britt Beemer & Robert Shook, William Morrow & Co. Inc.,
1997
ISBN: 0-688-14386-0

Reengineering the Corporation, Michael Hammer & James Champy, Harper Business,
1993
ISBN: 0-88730-640-3

Responsible Managers Get Results, Gerald W. Faust, Richard Lyles, Will Phillips,
AMACOM, 1988 ISBN: 0-8144-0389-1

Seven Habits of Highly Effective People, Stephen R. Covey, Fireside, 1990
ISBN: 0-671-70863-5

Sloan Management Review, The Delta Model: Adaptive Management for a Changing World,
Arnoldo C. Hax & Dean L Wilde II, Winter 1999, Vol 40, No. 2

The 21 Irrefutable Laws of Leadership, John C Maxwell, Thomas Nelson Inc.,
ISBN: 0-7852-7431-6

Transforming the Organization, Francis J. Goullart & James N. Kelly, McGraw- Hill,
Inc. 1995 ISBN: 0-07-034067-6

Webster's New World Dictionary, Simon & Schuster, 1989

Checklist/Criteria

AWARE: Team understands the tool or concept and knows how to implement.

USED: Team has used this tool or concept at least once

COMPETENT: Team has repeated experience with this tool or concept and see value in it

EXCELLENT: Team is self-directed with this tool or concept

Team Tools & Principles: This team utilizes a charter/mission statement to guide its actions. The team has regular meetings and follows the other meeting tools.				
	Aware	Used	Competent	Excellent
Charter/mission definition				
Roles & responsibilities				
Agenda & ground rules				
Problem-solving methodology				
Idea generation				
Recognition is used				
Team self surveys for improvement				

Customer Focus: This team conducted customer interviews, analyzed customer/supplier feedback, and established a continuous feedback system				
	Aware	Used	Competent	Excellent
Identify team's customers & contacts				
Identify products & services				
Obtain & analyze customer feedback				
Integrate customer requirements into performance measures				
Establish customer-supplier loops				
Use customer feedback in work process improvement efforts				

Process Management: This team has identified their key processes, analyzed them, mapped them, and implemented continuous improvement plans				
	Aware	Used	Competent	Excellent
Identify work processes				
Work process mapping				
Variance analysis				
Develop & implement process improvements				

Scorekeeping: This team has identified its key business and customer measures, had developed graphs to track those measures, and has developed action plans to improve those measures.

	Aware	Used	Competent	Excellent
Goals & measurements are defined				
A balanced scorecard is defined				
Scorecard is used to guide improvements				
Scorecard is monitored & changed as needed				
Team results are compared to expectations				
Benchmarking with other industries or firms				

Performance Improvement Results: This team has identified and solved problems, implemented improvement action plans, developed knowledge sharing of both success and failure, and has achieved measurable improvements.

	Aware	Used	Competent	Excellent
Demonstrates effective results				
Continuous improvement is ongoing, & a part of the management process				
Scorekeeping/ benchmarking is ongoing				
Results of action plans improve sales or profitability.				
Improved customer satisfaction surveys				
Innovation is encouraged, & supported				
Contributions to the whole organization is recognized & understood				
Team satisfaction				

About the author

Jack Veale, CMC, is a internationally recognized consultant, business strategist, and speaker who earned his BS in Business Administration from Norwich University in Northfield, Vermont, and his MBA from Boise State University, in Boise, Idaho. Jack is a certified Management Consultant with IMCUSA, and a Fellow of the family firm institute. Jack has assisted hundreds of companies in many industries and countries, offering solutions with strategic planning, succession planning, corporate governance, and crisis management. Jack is a nationally known speaker on privately held, ESOP, or family business issues, speaking specifically to the challenges their businesses face in this highly competitive environment. He has formed, and served on, several profit and non-profit boards, and has served as founder and President of the Connecticut Chapter of the National Association of Corporate Directors (NACD). He has been active in the Rotary Club International, Alliance of Mergers and Acquisition advisors, Attorneys for Family Held enterprises, as well as the Turnaround Management Association and many other associations. Jack and his wife, Laurie, have been married over 30 years, and have two children.

PTCFO, Inc.
48 Walkley Rd
West Hartford, CT 06119-1345

(860) 232-9858
(860) 232-9438 Fax
www.ptcfo.com

www.ingramcontent.com/pod-product-compliance
Lightning Source LLC
Chambersburg PA
CBHW081501200326
41518CB00015B/2336